The **Balanced** Reading Program

Helping All Students Achieve Success

Susan M. Blair-Larsen
The College of New Jersey
Ewing, New Jersey, USA

Kathryn A. Williams
Langston University
Langston, Oklahoma, USA

Editors

INTERNATIONAL
Reading
Association

800 Barksdale Road, PO Box 8139
Newark, Delaware 19714-8139, USA
www.reading.org

The International Reading Association attempts, through its publications, to provide a forum for a wide spectrum of opinions on reading. This policy permits divergent viewpoints without implying the endorsement of the Association.

Director of Publications   Joan M. Irwin
Assistant Director of Publications   Jeanette K. Moss
Editor in Chief, Books   Matthew W. Baker
Permissions Editor   Janet S. Parrack
Associate Editor   Tori Mello
Assistant Editor   Sarah Rutigliano
Acquisitions and Communications Coordinator   Amy T. Roff
Publications Coordinator   Beth Doughty
Association Editor   David K. Roberts
Production Department Manager   Iona Sauscermen
Art Director   Boni Nash
Electronic Publishing Supervisor   Wendy A. Mazur
Electronic Publishing Specialist   Anette Schütz-Ruff
Electronic Publishing Specialist   Cheryl J. Strum
Electronic Publishing Assistant   Peggy Mason

Project Editor   Matthew W. Baker

Library of Congress Cataloging in Publication Data
   The balanced reading program: Helping all students achieve success/Susan M. Blair-Larsen & Kathryn A. Williams, editors.
      p.   cm.
   Includes bibliographical references and indexes.
      1. Reading (Elementary)—United States.   2. Reading (Elementary)—United States case studies.   3. Classroom management—United States.   4. Curriculum planning—United States.   I. Blair-Larsen, Susan M.   II. Williams, Kathryn A. III. International Reading Association.
   LB1573.B3553   1999   99-37781
   372.4—dc21
   ISBN 0-87207-252-5

Second Printing, February 2000

Contents

Contributors

E. Jo Ann Belk
Associate Professor, Education
  Department
Mississippi State University,
  Meridian Campus
Meridian, Mississippi, USA

Susan M. Blair-Larsen
Associate Professor
The College of New Jersey
Ewing, New Jersey, USA

Eileen M. Burke
Professor
The College of New Jersey
Ewing, New Jersey, USA

Jan E. Hasbrouck
Assistant Professor
Texas A&M University
College Station, Texas, USA

Delores E. Heiden
Associate Professor of
  Reading Education
University of Wisconsin–
  La Crosse
La Crosse, Wisconsin, USA

William A. Henk
Director, School of Behavioral
  Sciences and Education
Penn State Harrisburg
Middletown, Pennsylvania, USA

Barbara A. Marinak
Reading/Federal Programs
  Coordinator
Central Dauphin School District
Harrisburg, Pennsylvania, USA

Milly Schrader
Principal
Elk Grove Unified School
  District
Elk Grove, California, USA

Dixie Lee Spiegel
Professor, Associate Dean for
  Students
School of Education
University of North Carolina at
  Chapel Hill
Chapel Hill, North Carolina,
  USA

Richard A. Thompson
Professor Emeritus
University of Central Florida
Orlando, Florida, USA

Kathryn A. Williams
Associate Professor
Langston University
Langston, Oklahoma, USA

Kerry M. Vallance
Reading Specialist
Centennial School District
Southampton, Pennsylvania,
USA

Introduction

Kathryn A. Williams and Susan M. Blair-Larsen

How children learn to read and how children should be taught to read are questions that for many years have intrigued both teachers and researchers. The search for answers to these questions stimulated a multiplicity of other questions and resulted in enduring pedagogical controversy over much of the 20th century. The most fervent and long lasting controversy has been the debate of phonics versus whole language as *the* way to teach reading acquisition. Proponents of phonics methods and proponents of whole language divided into two opposing camps. Controversy was so fierce that "war" was declared as leading proponents of each philosophy squared off in print. A great deal of effort was spent by both sides in describing the problems with the opposition's view. This added fuel to the controversy and further polarized both researchers and teacher practices. Fortunately, in recent years there has been considerable research progress in answering the questions posed about children's literacy development. Much has been learned about the basic processes that occur as part of learning to read. There is no longer any doubt that learning to read requires mastering the system by which print encodes the language. In an alphabetic orthography, such as English, this means the child must come to appreciate that the speech stream contains units that correspond to the symbols (letters and words) on the page.

Although there no longer is controversy over the importance of learning the principles of decoding to become a fluent reader, questions have remained about how teachers could and should make provisions for how the principles of decoding, particularly of the alphabetic principle, are acquired by the child. Other questions also have taken on new importance. Educators have asked, "In what ways do selection of materials to read, instructional approaches, teaching methodologies, and assessment tools influence the acquisition, proficiency, and quantity and quality of student engagement of reading?"

A great deal of thought and effort by researchers and teachers has been focused on this question of *how* reading should best be taught. Much of the search has been directed toward finding one particular answer for this multifaceted question—*the* best way to teach reading. This has led teachers back and forth, from one method of instruction to another, as each shows promise of being successful. Philosophical zeal has led to polarization of ideas and division of purpose among both teachers and researchers.

Concern that much of the controversy is counterproductive to, rather than contributing to finding an answer to how reading should best be taught has led educators to look at the theories, the research, and actual successful practices regarding the teaching of reading. Such contemplative study has led many to adopt a balanced perspective toward the question of how reading should best be taught.

A group of educators from the United Kingdom identified basic principles of balanced reading instruction in 1990. Since then, others in Australia, Canada, New Zealand, and the United States have come forth to discuss important issues of balance (see, for example, Freppon & Dahl, 1998; Iversen, 1994; Spiegel, 1998; Stahl, Duffy-Hester, & Stahl, 1998). These principles of balanced instruction, adopted officially at the initial meeting of the International Reading Association Balanced Reading Instruction Special Interest Group at the Association's 1993 Annual Convention, state that teachers wishing to achieve the highest rate of reading success for their students will continually seek to achieve balance in the following areas:

- balance between teaching students and facilitating their learning; that is, balancing teacher-directed explicit instruction and learner-centered discovery learning;

Kerry M. Vallance focus Chapter 3 on ways a teacher can balance comprehension instruction so students acquire a repertoire of effective strategies from which to draw when reading. The authors of this chapter provide charts, graphs, and other features to aid your implementation of balanced comprehension instruction.

In a balanced reading program, *what* is read is also of key importance. Skills taught are practiced and perfected through wide reading. Reading for pleasure and reading for fact are constant purposes for reading. In Chapter 4, Eileen M. Burke gives help in understanding the role of literature in a balanced reading program, specific suggestions for maximizing its use in practicing and perfecting skills, and suggestions on how to select appropriate, high-quality literature that gives maximum opportunity to help students grow into mature readers.

Effective teaching results from knowing your students, and assessment is a tool that allows teachers to acquire this knowledge. Delores E. Heiden offers valuable insight into the use of assessment in a balanced reading program in Chapter 5. She explains how to get started, what to do if you do not get the results you expected, and how to evaluate what you are doing. She describes several forms of assessment that can produce valuable data to inform your instruction, and she cautions about appropriate use of these and all assessment tools.

The next three chapters of the text offer descriptions of programs that exemplify a balanced approach. As you begin to make decisions about daily reading instruction and assessment for the purpose of achieving balance, you can read how others met the challenges encountered in the development of a balanced program. These chapters offer insight into major goals and explain the involvement of teachers, staff, administrators, community (parents), and students in program development. You will learn about specific classroom teaching strategies and materials, means to assess individual student progress, program evaluation, and anticipated changes in moving forward. These chapters will be particularly helpful for those who are struggling with change in their own classroom, trying to achieve an instructional balance that maximizes literacy success for all their students. In these, as in all the chapters, you will find details such as booklists, testing procedures, schedules, and forms to help you as you design your own balanced reading program.

In Chapter 6, E. Jo Ann Belk discusses the importance of early success in reading and how a balanced approach enables most children to acquire the necessary skills and the desire to read. The second part of this chapter, written from the viewpoint of a first-grade teacher, describes a balanced reading program designed for a first-grade class.

Chapter 7, written by Jan E. Hasbrouck and Milly Schrader, discusses how to implement a balanced beginning reading program in culturally diverse classrooms. This chapter considers the usual challenges involved with implementing program changes and discusses the vast range of needs increased diversity in student population brings. The authors describe how one school that was challenged with large numbers of children from culturally diverse, transient, and economically disadvantaged backgrounds teamed teachers, parents, and administrators to successfully implement an effective balanced reading program.

In Chapter 8, Barbara A. Marinak and William A. Henk give an enlightening account of how an entire school in a large suburban district made the transition to a balanced literacy program. This chapter highlights many of the basic components of the schoolwide program, then describes how the various elements are used to balance literacy instruction. This chapter is filled with valuable information for those striving for balance, including a discussion of the journey of the school's teachers through philosophy and methodology changes and how the changes in the reading program related to other school contexts.

Chapter 9 by Kathryn A. Williams concludes the book by summarizing and further clarifying some of the key elements of a balanced reading program. She also offers encouragement to those striving to implement their own program.

Choices must be made regarding what to include when planning a text of this size. We have chosen to offer a volume that clarifies the balanced reading perspective, gives a view of some of the elements of a balanced program, and gives those wishing to implement such a program insight into how balanced reading instruction is planned and how it looks when carried out in various classrooms. Phonological awareness and phonics instruction were not included as separate chapters because we believe the chapters describing actual programs best illustrate how, in a balanced reading program, the type, amount, and timing of such instruction may take place. We believe decisions regarding instruction must be based on analysis of group and individual needs and classroom circumstances and may be, as this book illustrates, resolved effectively in a variety of appropriate ways.

The contributors to this book are reading educators who believe in a balanced approach to reading instruction that is built on research, that views teachers as informed decision makers, and that is built on a comprehensive view of literacy. We intend this text to support teachers as they progress as decision makers and begin to implement change in their literacy instruction to achieve a more balanced and effective program that offers greater success to all their students.

REFERENCES

Adams, M.J. (1990). *Beginning to read: Thinking and learning about print.* Cambridge, MA: Massachusetts Institute of Technology Press.

Beck, I., & McKeown, M. (1991). Conditions of vocabulary acquisition. In R. Barr, M.L. Kamil, P. Mosenthal, & P.D. Pearson (Eds.), *Handbook of reading research: Volume II* (pp. 789–814). White Plains, NY: Longman.

Freppon, P.A., & Dahl, K.L. (1998). Balanced instruction: Insights and considerations. *Reading Research Quarterly, 33,* 240–251.

Heilman, A.W., Blair, T.R., & Rupley, W.H. (1998). *Principles and practices of teaching reading.* Upper Saddle River, NJ: Prentice Hall.

Iversen, S. (1994). Balanced reading instruction: What children need to know and how to teach it. *Balanced Reading Instruction, 1*(1), 21–30

Pearson, P.D., & Fielding, L. (1991). Comprehension instruction. In R. Barr, M.L. Kamil, P. Mosenthal, & P.D. Pearson, Eds., *Handbook of reading research: Volume II* (pp. 815–860). White Plains, NY: Longman.

Rupley, W.H., Logan, J.W., & Nichols, W.D. (1999). Vocabulary instruction in a balanced reading program. *The Reading Teacher, 55,* 338–355.

Spiegel, D.L. (1998). Silver bullets, babies, and bath water: Literature response groups in a balanced reading program. *The Reading Teacher, 52,* 114–124.

Stahl, S.A., Duffy-Hester, A., & Stahl, K. (1998). Everything you wanted to know about phonics (but were afraid to ask). *Reading Research Quarterly, 33,* 338–355

Walpole, S. (1999). Changing texts, changing thinking: Comprehension demands of new science textbooks. *The Reading Teacher, 52,* 358–369.

CHAPTER 1

The Perspective of the Balanced Approach

Dixie Lee Spiegel

Education often appears to be not just a field of dreams but a field of extremes. Literacy educators are not an exception to this tendency. In our quest to meet the increasingly complex needs of our students, we sometimes swing from one extreme to the next, searching for *the* way to educate children. Recently, however, a moderate perspective has gained visibility: Literacy educators are using the word *balanced* more and more. Could it be that we have finally realized that we are never going to find *the* way because there is no such thing as *the* learner, *the* task, or *the* curriculum? Could it be that at last we recognize that a middle position allows us to best serve the needs of all children as we draw judiciously from a broad spectrum of strategies for helping children develop their ability to read and write?

This book is about balance. Later chapters will present an explicit picture of how a balanced approach can be implemented in a school or classroom. This chapter serves as a foundation by defining what a balanced approach is and is not, discussing the importance of a balanced approach, suggesting why literacy education has not yet embraced the idea of a balanced approach, and presenting guidelines for developing and maintaining such an approach.

What a Balanced Approach Is and Is Not

To my delight, a recent buzzword in literacy education is *balanced*. Articles stressing balance now appear more often, sometimes written by individuals who in the past tended to express more focused views on how children's literacy development can be enhanced (for example, Strickland, 1996). There is growing evidence that elementary teachers, regardless of what philosophy or approach they claim to follow, actually take a more balanced approach than would be sanctioned by the advocates of their espoused more narrow approaches (Canney, 1993; Pressley, Rankin, & Yokoi, 1995).

But balance is too important a concept to be reduced to a catchy buzzword. We have seen what has happened to whole language: Some teachers studied the philosophy, attended workshops or even university classes, and implemented whole language philosophy in thoughtful ways. But others were attracted by pieces of the philosophy and proclaimed themselves to be whole language teachers primarily because they did not teach phonics or because they used children's trade books. Through their lack of understanding of a whole language approach, these latter teachers implemented a distorted and superficial view of this philosophy.

Similarly, some who espouse extreme phonics approaches have ignored the fact that most phonics advocates are adamant that phonics is but a part of a child's literacy program: The ability to use letter-sound relationships to identify unknown words for both reading and spelling is *part* of the set of word identification strategies a reader or writer needs, and word identification is *part* of the picture of literacy. Again, inappropriate implementation of a worthwhile idea has led to attack and dismissal of the entire original moderate point of view.

In order to avoid the tendency to latch on to yet another instructional concept superficially, it is important that we are clear about what a balanced approach is and is not. We have to agree on a definition, so the concept of balance is not subverted or trivialized.

A Balanced Approach Is Built on Research

A balanced approach is an approach, not a philosophy, built on sound research. And in the spirit of true scholarship, a balanced approach is built from an examination of a broad spectrum of research, taking into account all the evidence, not just evidence that supports a particular bias. Research shows clearly that almost every instructional approach works for some children (Adams, 1990; Bond & Dykstra, 1967; Pflaum, Walberg, Karegianes, & Rasher, 1980), but research also shows that no approach works for every child. For example, Reading Recovery releases children whom this extremely individualized program does not help after 60 lessons (Askew, Fountas, Lyons, Pinnell, & Schmitt, 1998). Delpit (1988) warns that African American children will often do better with explicit rather than indirect instruction. The First-Grade Studies (Bond & Dykstra, 1967) concluded that it is the teacher, not the approach, that is important, but this message seems to have been forgotten. So here is the message again: *Research shows that you can teach some of the children some of the time with one program or philosophy, but you cannot teach all the children all the time.* A balanced approach is built on this belief and bases the belief on a thorough examination of the extant research on literacy development, not just on a small subset of that research.

A Balanced Approach Is Built on a Comprehensive View of Literacy

Literacy is not solely word identification. Any program that attends only to word identification—especially a program that deals only with one word identification strategy, the use of phonics—cannot by definition be a balanced approach. Of course, word identification and phonics in particular must be part of a balanced approach. (See, for example, the work of Adams, 1990; Baumann & Ivey, 1997; Freppon & Dahl, 1991.)

Literacy is not solely constructing meaning. Any program that attends only to the construction of meaning, without attention to word identification, cannot by definition be a balanced approach. Of course, the construction of meaning must be part of a balanced approach. (See the work of Baumann & Ivey, 1997.)

Literacy is not solely loving reading and writing. Any program that attends only to enhancing children's enjoyment of and confidence in their own reading and writing cannot by definition be a balanced approach. Of course, the development of a love of reading and writing must be part of a balanced approach. (See the work of Freppon, 1992; Rosenblatt, 1978.)

And literacy is not just reading. It includes writing. Any literacy program that attends only to reading and ignores the reciprocal relationships between reading and writing development cannot by definition be a balanced approach. (See the work of Baumann & Ivey, 1997; Stotsky, 1983; Vacca & Rasinski, 1992.)

A Balanced Approach Is Flexible

Because research does not support the idea that one size fits all, that one approach will work with all children for all aspects of literacy development for all curricula, a balanced approach must be flexible. Teachers must examine all the alternatives and strive each day to find the best ways to help each child develop as a reader and a writer. This means that few approaches or strategies are automatically assumed appropriate for all children. It also means that few approaches or strategies are automatically rejected as never appropriate. Teachers need to have a firm understanding of a broad range of ways to enhance literacy development and have the wisdom and courage to try different approaches with different learners for different tasks. A balanced approach provides the ultimate expertise in "seizing the teachable moment" because the teacher has the knowledge and the flexibility to recognize a teachable moment and to draw from a wealth of strategies, not just one or two, to provide appropriate intervention. A teacher who follows a balanced approach also recognizes when no teaching is needed, when the best strategy is simply to get out of the way.

Flexibility should not be interpreted as trying to be all things to all people. Flexibility means empowerment. Teachers who implement a balanced approach are not flexible because they do not know what to do; they are flexible because they understand that there is not one best method of instruction. Teachers who strive to follow a balanced approach may be considered by many as more courageous, more intellectually rigorous, and more empowered than teachers who blindly follow a more narrow perspective.

A balanced approach sometimes has been described as a compromise position. However, compromise connotes that each side gives up something and the result is less than a whole. A compromise involves making the best of a bad situation when you cannot have it all your own way. Both parties lose something to get part of what they want rather than nothing—it is a lose/lose outcome. But a balanced approach is a synergistic position. The result is far more than the sum of its parts. Because the teacher is flexible and can draw from a plethora of strategies to tailor interactions with each learner, no one loses.

A Balanced Approach Is Built on a Realistic Picture of the Variety of Learners, Teachers, Curricula, and Schools

Authenticity is another buzzword that has become popular in recent years. Usually it refers to having children develop literacy through engagement in meaningful, often self-selected, tasks rather than through teacher-prepared interactions that may not relate to authentic uses of literacy. I would contend that a balanced approach is the most authentic way to enhance literacy development. A balanced approach is not based on a philosophy of what *ought* to be happening in schools or how children *ought* to learn. A balanced approach is not based on a vision of children who all learn in the same way and usually at the same time, or based on a picture of teachers who all have the same talents and personalities. A balanced approach *is* based on what goes on in each unique classroom with individual children and real teachers. It is based on an authentic and ecologically valid view of the variety of learners, teachers, curricula, and schools.

A Definition: A Balanced Approach Is

The aspects of balance just described lead to the following definition: A balanced approach is a decision-making approach through which a teacher makes thoughtful decisions each day about the best way to help each child become a better reader and writer. A balanced approach requires and enables a teacher to reflect on what he or she is doing and to modify instruction daily based on the needs of each individual learner. The modifications are drawn from a broad repertoire of strategies and a sound understanding of children, learning, and the theoretical bases of these strategies.

Why a Balanced Approach Is Important

In the earlier discussion of what a balanced approach is and is not, several points are made about why such an approach is important. Some of these points will be reviewed and expanded on in the following section, and additional points will be introduced.

Learners, Teachers, Curricula, and Schools Vary

There is no place where all children are the same and perfect. The incredible diversity of children in classrooms is part of what makes teaching exciting and constantly revitalizing. A balanced approach allows us to celebrate and draw from this natural diversity.

Because a balanced approach empowers teachers to select what is right for the ever-changing environment of their classrooms, teachers can be confident that they can come close to meeting the needs of each child. This flexibility helps to ensure that each child receives a developmentally appropriate education because he or she is viewed as an individual, not as a third grader or an earth science student or someone who is learning disabled. The flexibility inherent in a balanced approach gains increasing importance at higher grade levels as the variation among students increases and the tasks of school become more complex and challenging.

Children Deserve a Consistent Literacy Curriculum

A consistent but flexible curriculum seems to be an oxymoron, but it is not. Flexibility that moves outward from a small, consistent core curriculum allows teachers to meet the needs of each student across the grades in individualized ways. The key is avoiding the extremes of any unbalanced approach. When one teacher has a fairly limited approach, many children learn how to be "good" readers, writers, and learners only according to that teacher's narrow focus. For example, if the teacher espouses a whole language philosophy, then readers are rewarded for making intelligent guesses about words, constructing their own meanings, and selecting their own reading materials. As good writers in that classroom, the children use temporary spellings and attend more to the content of what they are writing than to the mechanics, especially in early drafts. Imagine the chaos the next year if these same children are in the classroom of a teacher who believes in the primacy of phonics and "getting it right." Children who were rewarded for taking risks are now labeled unsuccessful because accuracy, not approximation, is important. Listening to teacher explanations may replace student exploration. Academically talented children usually can survive this extreme shift in perspective, but less academically successful children may suffer from terminal whiplash. They had a hard enough time being successful with last year's teacher, and now much of what they were trying to learn to do is wrong; they have to learn a whole new curriculum and a whole new set of values about reading and writing. Their self-esteem, already low, plummets further. These children have been put at terrible jeopardy because their teachers had narrow, inflexible perspectives of what reading and writing are and how children become readers and writers.

A balanced approach helps to avoid the change inevitable in allowing each teacher to use his or her own approach, even if that approach is very different from any other teacher's. A balanced approach increases the likelihood that a whole-school literacy program can be developed that accommodates the beliefs and styles of most of the school's teachers. A balanced approach does not require capitulation to someone else's perspective in order to adopt a program to which the entire school can adhere. Rather, a balanced approach allows a faculty to agree on a small core of principles about teaching and learning and a small core of curriculum around which each teacher can individualize. Thus, one part of the core for an elementary school might be a set of word identification strategies (for example, use of context, onset and rime, phonics, and structural analysis) on which all teachers would agree to ensure that their students learned. How the teachers assisted their students in learning and applying these strategies and the degree to which each strategy was emphasized would vary from classroom to classroom and child to child because of the flexibility built into a balanced approach. But children from grade to grade would have the same concept of how a good reader identifies words.

Programs That Lack Balance Invite Attack and Interference

Programs that lack balance are not successful with all children. Therefore they invite attack, which often takes the form of suggesting that the pendulum swing all the way to an equally unbalanced program of an opposite stance. An unbalanced program presents a clear target for the disenchanted and mobilizes most effectively those who espouse the opposite approach. This was evident in the reaction to the failure of adherence to basal reading programs to meet all children's needs; the solution was to move to whole language. Now that whole language also has failed to be the solution to all problems, we find strident voices insisting that the panacea is phonics.

On the other hand, a balanced approach is likely to have some aspects that make supporters of both approaches happy, and therefore suggestions for change are likely to be more moderate. A balanced approach is not demonized by those who do not like it, because it does have some aspects of which most literacy educators approve. Therefore modification seems to be more a matter of fine-tuning and changing emphases than starting over from an entirely different perspective.

Unbalanced programs also leave schools open to attack from outside forces, primarily legislators. Because such programs fail, legislators are unhappy. Because few legislators also are informed literacy educators, they tend to look for simplistic answers. For example, "If *A* doesn't work (and they can figure out what *A* is because it is so limited) then let's try *Z* (which is the opposite, equally limited, and therefore easily identified)." Many legislators lack the sophistication to intuitively understand more balanced positions. Furthermore, those who believe in less balanced approaches often promote their positions fervently. Thus proponents of more limited instructional approaches are more likely than individuals espousing balanced stances to have a group identity and be ready to take action to gain the ear of legislators. Balanced approaches have the potential to limit legislative interference not only because they are more likely to be successful with more children but also because they do not seduce lawmakers into thinking they know enough to interfere. It is not as easy to see the "one other way of doing it" when a balanced approach is used.

Why We Do Not Already Have Balanced Programs Everywhere

A balanced approach seems so reasonable, so adaptable, that it amazes me that it has not been universally endorsed and put into practice. It is important to explore possible impediments to the adoption of a balanced approach in order to find out and hopefully remove the obstacles to its acceptance and implementation.

The Search for the "Silver Bullet"

Sad to say, literacy education is not immune to dreams of finding *the* answer, the silver bullet that will slay the monster of illiteracy and make success available to all. Absolutes are very attractive. They bring a false sense of closure, security, and control. But education absolutes are almost always based in part on false premises. There is enough truth in them to make their claims ring true, but careful examination of the assumptions of their absolutist positions show their faulty foundations.

Take, for example, the position that if children can just learn to "break the code" through phonics, they will be successful readers (Flesch, 1955). We will call this the *phonics position*, to distinguish it from the balanced position that phonics is an important but not sufficient part of most children's literacy development. The phonics position is attractive because it is simple and concrete: Here is what children need to learn to become readers and here are the materials to teach them. The phonics position also is attractive because it is supported by research: Children can learn phonics and can use this knowledge to identify unknown words (or pseudowords) (Adams, 1990). The phonics position draws from our natural desires for simple, manageable answers. It is also attractive to some administrators and legislators because it appears to be "teacher proof."

But the phonics position is not the silver bullet, the one answer. It is based on faulty assumptions. Reading is not just decoding words. It is primarily constructing meaning, and access to the words that help to convey meaning is only part of reading. Further, phonics is only one key to decoding. Using context and structural analysis are also important strategies. The phonics position deals with only one small part of literacy development. In this case simple is actually simplistic.

On the other hand, some have heralded whole language as the solution that will give all children access to literacy. As with phonics, there is a moderate view of whole language that has characteristics of a balanced approach. This moderate view permits flexibility and is based on a comprehensive concept of literacy. But as with phonics, there is also a camp that is more absolutist. This *whole-only position* is attractive because it paints a lovely picture: Children are exploring happily, teachers are guiding, and everyone is feeling good about themselves as readers and writers. The whole-only position is attractive because it focuses on the construction of meaning and the enjoyment of reading and writing. It is the whole, not the parts (words, sounds, letters) that is important in literacy. The whole-only position is attractive because it views literacy development as natural: Children will learn to read in the same way they learn oral language, naturally through social interaction, authentic situations, and without direct instruction. The whole-only position is attractive because it emphasizes teacher empowerment: Rather than focusing on materials to teach literacy, this position relies on teachers as intelligent decision makers who base their decisions on "kid watching."

But like the phonics position, the whole-only position is also flawed. Not all children learn through self-directed exploration (Delpit, 1988). Significant differences exist between oral language and written language that mean learning to read and write varies in important ways from learning to speak and listen (Adams, 1990). And in the construction of meaning from print and the conveyance of meaning through print, inattention to individual words and letters often leads to incorrect construction of meaning or ineffective writing. Thus the whole-only position is not the silver bullet.

Other Impediments to Implementing a Balanced Program

One major impediment is ignorance. A balanced approach requires a clear understanding of a variety of approaches, strategies, and viewpoints. When teachers do not fully understand alternatives, they cannot intelligently implement, modify, or reject them. The more broad teachers' understanding is, the more complete their repertoire will be and the more successful their balanced approach will be.

Lack of a clear understanding may lead to inappropriate implementation, and therefore premature dismissal of a strategy. A teacher once told me that she had tried literature circles in her class one day and they did not work. The children could not discuss what they had read. So now that teacher has rejected the idea of literature circles, probably forever. I would contend that her failure to understand the importance of a move into literature circles by planned stages over several weeks caused her to reject an activity that has the potential to enhance her students' literacy growth immeasurably. Because she implemented the activity inappropriately, her balanced program was diminished because she narrowed her options.

A related impediment is overreaction to failure. Sometimes when an activity or an approach has not worked well, the tendency is to move as far away from that approach as possible. For example, if a heavy emphasis on phonics has not led all children to become successful readers, we should get rid of all phonics. If whole language has not led all children to become successful readers, we should go back to phonics only. Life is rarely either/or; it is usually a continuum of options. A pendulum reaction that scythes from one end of the continuum to the other without a break dichotomizes literacy education and makes a balanced approach impossible. Again, the options have been narrowed to only two, but there is ample evidence that the two extremes do not meet the needs of all children.

Personality is yet another impediment for some individuals. Some individuals will find it difficult to move toward a balanced approach because they are resistant to change. Change is threatening ("But what if the new way is even worse? What if I can't do it?"); it rocks the boat ("Things aren't so bad. I like what I do. All my materials are developed."); and it requires hard work ("I already spend every evening preparing for the next day. When am I going to learn how to make these changes and develop all these new materials?"). For these individuals, it is easier to keep doing what they have been doing. A balanced approach requires daily change, which can be very unsettling for some educators.

On the other hand, some individuals will espouse enthusiastically any new idea that passes by. Without a clear understanding of what they are accepting, without reflection, they buy wholesale an approach or a philosophy just because it is new or appears to be new. Instead of considering how they might incorporate these new ideas into a balanced approach, these individuals throw away the old and replace it with the new or at least their concept of the new until the next new idea comes along.

Finally, a serious impediment is outside interference (Pearson, 1996). I have already discussed the tendency for some legislatures, state departments of public instruction, and administrators to be seduced by simple solutions. Simple solutions are rarely if ever balanced. Balance by its very nature is neither simple nor tidy. It is imperative that legislators and others in positions of power be educated to understand the importance of balance and to abandon their own search for one solution to children's reading problems.

Most of the impediments described here can be removed or at least minimized by thoughtful literacy educators working and learning together. No one person is going to find *the* answer, but we all can learn by studying and celebrating what has worked for others. In that way we can broaden our own repertoires, our own options, so that we can better meet the needs of each child.

How to Establish and Maintain Balance

A balanced approach can be daunting simply because there is no right answer. It is the teacher who must watch each child with each task and be able to determine what the child is using successfully, using but confusing (Invernizzi, 1995), and not using at all. It is the teacher who must search his or her repertoire of strategies and decide what to try next when a child has not achieved success. It is the teacher who must decide how each child best learns. The questions that follow are designed to help teachers gain control over these crucial decisions.

Do I Have a Comprehensive View of Literacy?

■ Am I including both reading and writing?

■ For reading, am I including comprehension, the construction of meaning?

■ For reading, am I including word identification?

■ For writing, am I including an emphasis on ideas, not just mechanics?

- For writing, am I also including an emphasis on mechanics in final drafts after Grade 1?
- Am I fostering enjoyment of reading and writing?
- Do I overemphasize any one facet of literacy?
- Do I take into consideration the variety of authentic uses of reading and writing?

Do I Have a Clear Understanding of a Broad Range of Options for Promoting Literacy Development?

- Do I understand the research that supports various options?
- Have I considered using both direct instruction and learner-directed discovery, and do I understand when each is appropriate?
- Have I considered using both whole texts and pieces of text (for example, isolated phrases, words, sounds), and do I understand when each is appropriate?
- Have I considered using both portfolio assessment and standardized assessment, and do I understand when each is appropriate?
- Am I aware of a variety of strategies for word identification, and do I help children to apply these strategies?
- Am I aware of a variety of strategies for constructing meaning, and do I help children apply these strategies?
- Am I aware of a variety of strategies for promoting effective writing?

Can I Match Children With Strategies?

- Am I able to determine what strategies children are using successfully, using but confusing, and not using at all?
- Do I have a system that helps me keep track of each child's literacy development?

Do I Truly Believe in a Balanced Approach?

- Am I open to new ideas?

- Do I reject ideas only after adequate evidence or reflection?
- Do I adhere to ideas only after adequate evidence or reflection?
- Am I always looking for what is working and what is not working and seeking alternatives?
- Do I truly believe that there is not one best approach?

Conclusion

As literacy educators we need to stop the search for *the* answer to effective literacy instruction. We need to acknowledge and even celebrate the natural diversity of learners, schools, teachers, and curricula that exists. We need to open our minds to learn from others and to reflect on what we think we already know. And we need to have the courage and self-confidence to believe that we can decide what is best for each child each day. A balanced program will do all this for us, and most importantly, for children.

REFERENCES

Adams, M.J. (1990). *Beginning to read: Thinking and learning about print.* Cambridge, MA: Massachusetts Institute of Technology Press.

Askew, B., Fountas, I., Lyons, C., Pinnell, G., & Schmitt, M. (1998). *Reading Recovery review: Understandings outcomes and implications.* Columbus, OH: Reading Recovery Council of North America.

Baumann, J., & Ivey, G. (1997). Delicate balances: Striving for curricular and instructional equilibriums in a second-grade, literature/strategy-based classroom. *Reading Research Quarterly, 32,* 244–275.

Bond, G.L., & Dykstra, R. (1967). The cooperative research program in first-grade reading instruction. *Reading Research Quarterly, 2,* 5–142.

Canney, G. (1993). Teachers' preferences for reading materials. *Reading Improvement, 30,* 238–245.

Delpit, L.D. (1988). The silenced dialogue: Power and pedagogy in educating other people's children. *Harvard Educational Review, 58,* 280–298.

Flesch, R. (1955). *Why Johnny can't read and what you can do about it.* New York: Harper & Row.

Freppon, P. (1992). Difficulties in evaluation in a traditional U.S. school. In C. Bouffler (Ed.), *Literacy evaluation: Issues and practicalities* (pp. 21–27). Newtown, Australia: Primary English Teaching Association.

Freppon, P., & Dahl, K. (1991). Learning about phonics in a whole language class-room. *Language Arts, 69,* 192–200.

Invernizzi, M. (1995). *Finding the balance with reading and spelling.* Paper present-ed at the 40th Annual Convention of the International Reading Association, Anaheim, CA.

Pearson, P.D. (1996). Six ideas in search of a champion: What policymakers should know about the teaching and learning of literacy in our schools. *Journal of Literacy Research, 28,* 302–309.

Pflaum, S.W., Walberg, H.J., Karegianes, M.L., & Rasher, S.P. (1980). Reading in-struction: A quantitative analysis. *Educational Researcher, 9,* 12–18.

Pressley, M., Rankin, J., & Yokoi, L. (1995). *A survey of instructional practices of primary teachers nominated as effective in promoting literacy* (Reading Research Report No. 41). Athens, GA: National Reading Research Center.

Rosenblatt, L. (1978). *The reader, the text, the poem.* Carbondale, IL: Southern Illinois University Press.

Stotsky, S. (1983). Research on reading/writing relationships: A synthesis and sug-gested directions. *Language Arts, 60,* 627–643.

Strickland, D.S. (1996, October/November). In search of balance: Restructuring our literacy programs. *Reading Today,* p. 32.

Vacca, R., & Rasinski, T. (1992). *Case studies in whole language.* Fort Worth, TX: Harcourt Brace.

CHAPTER 2

Balancing Vocabulary Instruction With Teacher-Directed and Student-Centered Activities

Richard A. Thompson

Understanding what one reads is dependent on a number of reading skills, prior knowledge, and especially vocabulary. Reading vocabulary translates into reading power. Identification and understanding the meaning of words accounts for a significant portion of a reader's ability to comprehend a given selection (Anderson & Freebody, 1979; Beck, Perfetti, & McKeown, 1982; Jenkins, Pany, and Schreck, 1978). The effect of vocabulary knowledge on comprehension ability would be difficult to overestimate. By integrating both teacher-directed and student-centered learning activities into a reading vocabulary instruction program, a teacher will provide balanced instruction for students' reading vocabulary acquisition.

Research and Background Information on Vocabulary Knowledge

Reading educators agree that vocabulary knowledge begets reading power, because a reader's understanding comes chiefly from his or her vocabulary base. Vocabulary can be learned through reading, by being instructed, and by pursuing student-centered activities. Teachers striving to offer their students a balance of instructional techniques infuse direct instruction of vocabulary and student-centered activities into their reading programs to balance the vocabulary growth implicit in whole-reading activities. The question that must be addressed is how to balance vocabulary instruction to best serve students.

Some educators suggest that readers should skip unknown words encountered in their reading. Although excellent readers of all ages do skip unknown words and can derive understanding from the print they are able to read, they have the metacognitive awareness to know when to retreat and reread or find the meaning in a source. Research explicitly states that for beginning readers and those of all ages who are not facile readers, skipping unknown words in running text matters greatly (see, for example, Adams, 1990). The short-term effect will be inaccurate understanding of the printed material and the long-term effect will be the inculcation of a negative reading strategy. Ekwall and Shanker (1985) are direct on this point: "Make students aware of new words when they read and teach students not to skip them" (p. 263).

In her book *Beginning to Read: Thinking and Learning About Print*, Adams (1990) reinforces the notion of readers addressing all words. Although learning vocabulary from context is a very important component of vocabulary acquisition, Adams makes it clear that it is only effective if children engage in meaningful reading and, even then, only if they attempt to process the spelling—the orthographic structure—of the unknown words. She writes, "Where they skip over an unknown word without attending to it, and often readers do, no learning can occur" (p. 150). Adams recommends that readers practice "using not just the drift of the context but also looking for definitions, paraphrases, and contrasts that follow or more remotely precede the word" (p. 153). Vocabulary growth occurs as students read, but only if unknown words are made known. A wise teaching strategy is to preteach unknown words to students before they encounter them in their reading and to use the running text as reinforcement.

Researchers (Anderson & Freebody, 1981; Davis, 1944; Spearitt, 1972; Thurstone, 1946) have connected vocabulary knowledge with readers' comprehension abilities. Stahl and Fairbanks (1986) treated the accumulated vocabulary research to meta-analysis. Their analysis led them to conclude that teaching vocabulary increases students' word knowledge and comprehension abilities. Johnson and Pearson (1984) noted that there is agreement among reading teachers, educators, and researchers that fluent reading and vocabulary size are correlated positively and that children who do not know many words or who have not acquired the means of learning new words cannot read very well. This positive and reciprocal relation between vocabulary knowledge and comprehension power clearly indicates that reading vocabulary instruction should be practiced by all teachers, regardless of grade or subject area.

Though the causal relation between vocabulary knowledge and comprehension has been verified repeatedly, not all reading teachers realize the importance vocabulary learning has to reading fluency and understanding what is read. Durkin's (1979) classic study dealt partly with the following question: Do reading teachers teach vocabulary? Durkin concluded that for the 4,469 minutes of reading instruction denoted by her observers, only 19 minutes involved direct vocabulary teaching. Roser and Juel (1982) observed third-, fourth-, and fifth-grade teachers and found that they spent an average of 1.67 minutes on vocabulary per reading lesson, and what was even more worrisome, most often teachers were spending no time on vocabulary instruction. These studies indicate there are many teachers who are not teaching vocabulary or who minimize vocabulary instruction apparently not realizing the relation between vocabulary knowledge and comprehension power. Knowledge of this strong relation should motivate teachers to provide vocabulary instruction in their reading classes as well as providing vocabulary foundations in every subject area.

Where Should Vocabulary Instruction Be Inserted in the Curriculum?

The demonstrated positive relation between vocabulary knowledge and comprehension ability makes the teaching of vocabulary a prime instructional task, but where should vocabulary instruction be transacted? Vocabulary instruction belongs in every reading program and in all curriculum subjects. The job for elementary teachers is to systematically teach vocabulary in their reading programs and in the subjects they teach, while subject specialists have the responsibility of teaching vocabulary related to their disciplines. The positive relation vocabulary has to comprehension commands that students be given vocabulary instruction frequently, if not daily.

Vocabulary instruction can be delivered in several ways. Teachers using commercial reading programs usually introduce vocabulary before having students read a story. This practice not only ensures that new vocabulary has been seen by readers, but it can help establish a story's setting, helping readers tune into what is coming in the story. After a story is read, vocabulary reinforcement is appropriate. Following up with questions about the previously introduced vocabulary and nonintroduced new vocabulary encountered in the story are timely and productive activities. After group activities such as working on crossword puzzles or magic squares, the time is ideal for additional vocabulary learning. Before visiting places such as museums, fire stations, or courthouses, teachers can introduce vocabulary of what will be seen and follow up on these terms when returning to the classroom. Teachers also can have "show and tell" activities first thing in the morning. Besides meeting other objectives, these are excellent vocabulary-building experiences. Before any experiences outside the typical classroom curriculum, such as films or a visiting speaker, teachers should preteach the vocabulary. Also, before students read columns from the newspaper in paper form or on the computer, teachers should target direct vocabulary instruction. Opportunities for vocabulary instruction abound; hardly any instructional activity can pay such high dividends in relation to time spent as teacher-directed vocabulary instruction.

Guiding Principles for Vocabulary Instruction

Beck and McKeown (1991) give four principles to guide teachers in meeting the vocabulary needs of their students.

1. All teaching approaches yield greater vocabulary growth than no instruction.

2. No one tactic has been found to be invariably better than others.

3. There is a benefit to instruction that includes a diversity of techniques.

4. Repeated exposures to words are profitable. (p. 805)

A diversity of techniques and repeated exposures to words are important concepts for teachers to implement. The thrust of this chapter is to help teachers diversify their vocabulary instruction and provide repeated vocabulary exposure. These means are carried out by balancing teacher-directed instruction and student-centered learning opportunities. Both types of activities can be implemented to spark students' interests and help them acquire reading vocabulary.

Teacher-Directed Vocabulary Activities

McCormick (1995) notes that authorities do not agree on all aspects of how word meanings are most likely to be learned, but there is a strong consensus on the value of direct instruction to facilitate indepth understanding of word meanings. Effective teachers provide a balanced approach in their planning and consider individual student differences, because not all students need the same instruction. These teachers also realize that vocabulary instruction improves comprehension best when the vocabulary words are presented in more than one context. Examples of teacher-directed vocabulary activities are preteaching vocabulary before reading lessons and content-area reading assignments, and employing semantic mapping (both these activities are discussed in this section). Other activities not discussed at length here include Vocabulary-Oral Language-Prediction (VLP) (see Wood & Robinson, 1983) and others listed in Tierney, Readence, and Dishner's *Reading Strategies and Practices* (1990). The following activities are meant to be helpful for teacher planning in meeting the diverse needs of students and will deliver more learning value than having students look up words and put them into sentences.

Preteaching Reading Vocabulary

Vocabulary introduction promotes readiness for reading. As Dechant (1993) notes, readers' schemata are enlarged with the development of vocabulary concepts. An important practice of expanding children's schemata is the preteaching of words that the student cannot identify or will likely be unable to recognize in a forthcoming reading selection. To make use of their personal schemata for implementing predictive strategies, readers must be able to identify and recode most of the words. Roser and Juel (1982) found that preteaching new vocabulary terms can result in significant gains in comprehension, and it affects students' abilities to read fluently. Teaching vocabulary prior to students' reading independently helps prevent readers from encountering roadblocks as they move along the print paths that lead to understanding. Although preteaching vocabulary has long been a part of teachers' instructional reading tactics and has been effective for many years, Durkin (1984) notes that many teachers are not establishing backgrounds for their readers. Many teachers have been misled into using a nonteaching, nonlearning strategy in which they believe all they have to do is put books into students' hands and the readers' prior experiences will enable them to read, and that if the readers cannot identify a word they should skip it. Skipping unknown words cannot teach students anything. Preteaching vocabulary is instruction, and is superior to the nonlearning strategy of telling students to skip words.

Semantic Mapping

Before students are to read a story, the teacher can direct a semantic mapping lesson enabling students to build their reading vocabularies. Heilman, Blair, and Rupley (1998) recommend the following procedure.

1. The teacher chooses a word from the story and writes it on the chalkboard or chart.

2. By brainstorming with students, related words are written on the board.

3. Categorization of the words follows and the additional words essential to the story are added to the appropriate categories. (p. 208)

Semantic mapping is a viable prereading vocabulary builder. It is a prelude to finding these words in context. Students are ordinarily fascinated by new words and thrive on immediate application of their new-found word knowledge. Students quickly learn that this teaching strategy increases their word banks.

Although direct instruction of vocabulary profits students' reading power, teachers who reinforce their direct instruction with student-centered learning activities will help strengthen vocabulary learning while adding more words to students' reading vocabularies. These activities include many opportunities for reading library and textbooks, solving crossword puzzles, and completing magic squares.

Student-Centered Vocabulary Activities

Wide Reading

One of the most important student-centered vocabulary learning activities is wide reading. Therefore, students need to have many opportunities to read independently. Reading educators agree that wide reading opportunities provide vocabulary learning opportunities for students. Although there are many ways to improve students' vocabularies, probably none are as easy and effective as reading programs that provide for a great deal of silent reading (Ekwall & Shanker, 1985).

Ordinarily, students read widely because they have the reading skills to cope with the print. Poor readers do not read widely. With poor and slow readers, it is vital that teachers provide appropriate reading material that is well within the reading competence of the student. The second important item is to provide interesting material to read. Interest and ability to read print are the keys to successful reading for every student, and these are especially crucial for poor readers. As Gunning (1998) notes, students need not read only books; any reading material meeting the reading level and interest of the student can be instructional, including newspapers, comic books, recipes, magazines, or how-to manuals.

Learning to recognize and know the meaning of words is a means to understanding the message conveyed by the author. Increasing sight vocabularies and print processing opportunities are mutually reinforcing, positively affecting reading power. Students acquire vocabulary as they process print by seeing meaningful words in proper contexts. The contextual situation often helps the reader to unlock an unknown word. Although direct instructional tactics are effective in increasing students' visual vocabularies and should be employed assiduously, reading experiences will provide word identification practice and will lead to reading vocabulary growth for students. Teachers must motivate students to read in the classroom and after school. Getting students to voraciously process print is a sure-fire, student-centered vocabulary builder.

Learning Activities With Puzzles and Squares

A reading teacher who can connect pleasure with learning makes a strong contribution to his or her students' learning futures. Fun learning activities enable a teacher to make this connection because they motivate students. Incremental but daily fun activities will accumulate and pay dividends of increased reading power. Contests and games are effective learning activities because they provide a change of pace and are as suitable for vocabulary development as they are for other instructional activities. Many reading games can be found in teacher resource books such as *Learning Activities for Reading* (Herr, 1982) and *Remediating Reading Difficulties* (Crawley & Merritt, 1995).

If everyone has a chance to win, games sustain students' motivation. Because there are many differences among student abilities, a teacher can allow every participant a chance to win by assigning students to teams of comparable ability.

Although games are certainly useful in helping students learn vocabulary, these activities alone will not likely be as effective as when they are used in conjunction with other vocabulary learning strategies. Fun activities such as crossword puzzles and magic squares are most effective in helping students improve their reading comprehension when these tactics are used in conjunction with reading the words in context, processing them in writing, and having multiple exposures to them. As Stahl (1986) notes, "vocabulary instruction improves comprehension only when both definitions and context are given, and has the largest effect when a number of different activities or examples using the word in context are used" (p. 663). Repetition is the oldest law of learning and is still a most important learning strategy especially when learning to process the printed word. Therefore, providing multiple tactics for students to encounter and process the vocabulary words deemed important for learning is a dynamic teaching strategy. The following student-centered learning activities can play important roles in students' vocabulary acquisition.

Crossword puzzles

Crossword puzzles can be excellent vocabulary builders. Students usually find they are interesting and fun, and puzzles do not necessarily have to be finished on school time. However, the puzzles can be fun and interesting only if they are within the students' competency levels. Otherwise, they become assignments of frustration and can have a negative impact on students' motivation for learning vocabulary. Because one puzzle will not ordinarily match everyone's ability level, making several puzzles with different numbers of blanks helps teachers individualize their student-centered crossword puzzle activities. Puzzles of 5, 15, and 30 word blanks can be made. Students who finish a puzzle early can go on to other puzzles or can be challenged to create their own puzzle for use by other cooperative learners.

There is no secret or easy way to make crossword puzzles. Crossword puzzles were introduced in the early 1900s, but the only task that is easier now is drawing lines with the computer. Puzzle creators begin by working horizontally. They put in all the words going across, working downward on succeeding lines until they finish the bottom line. Next, they put in the vertical words up and down across the puzzle moving from left to right. In short, when making your own puzzle put in the horizontal items first and then the vertical items. Blacken in spaces between words and do not worry about constructing puzzles as tidy as the ones in newspapers. Attractiveness is nice, but it is unrelated to the value of this learning activity. Leaving many blank spaces will not detract from the puzzle's value to your students.

Once you have made puzzles and found how successfully they motivate and help students learn, consider having students create their own puzzles by hand or with the aid of computers. Puzzle making is an excellent cooperative learning activity that can use vocabulary words from any subject area.

Magic squares

Rather than having students respond to a reading vocabulary worksheet or a chalkboard activity related to a reading worksheet, try using a magic square (see Figure on next page). A magic square functions in any way you would use a crossword puzzle, and it's easy to make up.

In the context of this chapter, magic squares are usable as pre- and postassessors of vocabulary. Rather than checking vocabulary knowledge with multiple choice and matching items, consider using magic squares. Perhaps they are no better than multiple choice items, but they are different, and under testing conditions, something different might be greatly welcomed by your students. If the magic square seems to ameliorate testing anxiety and even promote an element of fun, then perhaps the testing time will be tolerated more easily. A magic square has a mysterious quality revealed only when all the statements are matched correctly to their related words or phrases contained within the cells of the square. When the numbers add up to the magic number, the student knows the answers are correct.

Figure
Magic Squares

9-Cell Square

4	3	8
9	5	1
2	7	6

Magic number is 15

16-Cell Square

1	15	14	4
12	6	7	9
8	10	11	5
13	3	2	16

Magic number is 34

25-Cell Square

3	16	9	22	15
20	8	21	14	2
7	25	13	1	19
24	12	5	18	6
11	4	17	10	23

Magic number is 65

Concluding Thoughts

Vocabulary knowledge positively impacts on students' comprehension, because reading vocabularies are the building blocks of students' comprehension abilities and positively build students' comprehension power. This causal relation means that teachers can improve students' comprehension abilities by planting vocabulary in students' minds. These seeds will sprout and grow, providing students with concepts needed to think and learn about print.

Teachers who provide balanced vocabulary instruction are more likely to meet the vocabulary needs of their students as opposed to those teachers who think vocabulary can be learned well enough just from whole-reading activities. This balanced vocabulary instruction can help teachers provide a balance in their entire reading program.

REFERENCES

Adams, M.J. (1990). *Beginning to read: Thinking and learning about print.* Cambridge, MA: Massachusetts Institute of Technology Press.

Anderson, R.C., & Freebody, P. (1979). *Vocabulary knowledge and reading* (Reading Education Report No. 11). Urbana, IL: University of Illinois, Center for the Study of Reading. (ERIC Document Reproduction Service No. ED 177470)

Anderson, R., & Freebody, P. (1981). Vocabulary knowledge. In J.T. Guthrie (Ed.), *Comprehension and teaching: Research reviews* (pp. 77–117). Newark, DE: International Reading Association.

Beck, I., & McKeown, M. (1991). Conditions of vocabulary acquisition. In R. Barr, M.L. Kamil, P. Mosenthal, & P.D. Pearson (Eds.), *Handbook of reading research: Volume II* (pp. 789–814). White Plains, NY: Longman.

Beck, I.L., Perfetti, C.A., & McKeown, M.G. (1982). Effects of long-term vocabulary instruction on lexical access and reading comprehension. *Journal of Educational Psychology, 74,* 506–521.

Crawley, S.J., & Merritt, K. (1995). *Remediating reading difficulties* (2nd ed.). New York: Brown Benchmark.

Davis, F. (1944). Fundamental factors of comprehension in reading. *Psychometrika, 9,* 185–197.

Dechant, E. (1993). *Whole-language reading: A comprehensive teaching guide.* Lancaster, PA: Technomic.

Durkin, D. (1979). What classroom observations reveal about reading comprehension instruction. *Reading Research Quarterly, 14,* 481–533.

Durkin, D. (1984). Is there a match between what elementary teachers do and what basal reader manuals recommend? *The Reading Teacher, 37,* 734–744.

Ekwall, E.E., & Shanker, J.L. (1985). *Teaching reading in the elementary school* (2nd ed.). Columbus, OH: Merrill.

Gunning, T.G. (1998). *Assessing and correcting reading and writing difficulties.* Boston, MA: Allyn & Bacon.

Heilman, A.W., Blair, T.R., & Rupley, W.H. (1998). *Principles and practices of teaching reading* (9th ed.). Upper Saddle River, NJ: Prentice Hall.

Herr, S.E. (1982). *Learning activities for reading* (4th ed.). New York: William C. Brown.

Jenkins, J.R., Pany, D., & Schreck, J. (1978). *Vocabulary and reading comprehension: Instructional effects* (Technical Report No. 100). Urbana, IL: University of Illinois, Center for the Study of Reading. (ERIC Document Reproduction Service No. ED 160 999)

Johnson, D.D., & Pearson, P.D. (1984). *Teaching reading vocabulary* (2nd ed.). New York: Holt, Rinehart and Winston.

McCormick, S. (1995). *Instructing students who have literacy problems* (2nd ed.). Englewood Cliffs, NJ: Prentice Hall.

Roser, N., & Juel, C. (1982). Effects of vocabulary instruction on reading comprehension. In J.A. Niles & L.A. Harris (Eds.), *New inquiries in reading research
and instruction: Thirty-first yearbook of the National Reading Conference* (pp.
110–118). Rochester, NY: National Reading Conference.

Spearitt, D. (1972). Identification of subskills in reading comprehension by maximum likelihood factor analysis. *Reading Research Quarterly, 8*, 92–111.

Stahl, S. (1986). Three principles of effective vocabulary instruction. *Journal of
Reading, 29*, 662-668.

Stahl, S., & Fairbanks, M. (1986). The effects of vocabulary instruction: A model-
based meta-analysis. *Review of Educational Research, 56*(1), 72–110.

Thurstone, L. (1946). A note on a reanalysis of Davis' reading tests. *Psychometrika,
11*, 185–188.

Tierney, R., Readence, J., & Dishner, E. (1990). *Reading strategies and practices*
(3rd ed.). Boston, MA: Allyn & Bacon.

Wood, K.D., & Robinson, N. (1983). Vocabulary, language, and prediction: A prereading strategy. *The Reading Teacher, 36*, 392–395.

CHAPTER 3

■ ■ ■

Comprehension Instruction in a Balanced Reading Classroom

Susan M. Blair-Larsen and Kerry M. Vallance

Comprehension is a multidimensional thinking process; it is the interaction of the reader, the text, and the context. Comprehension is a strategic process by which readers construct meaning from written text. It is a complex skill requiring the coordination of a number of interrelated sources of information (Anderson, Hiebert, Scott, & Wilkinson, 1985).

In order for comprehension to occur, readers make critical connections between their prior knowledge and new-found knowledge in the text. When the connection is made, the understanding of the text is completely individual because interpretation is unique to the reader. While reading a text, readers activate their prior knowledge (schemata) about a topic. Readers use both their schemata and clues from the text as they comprehend (Spiro, 1979, as cited in Burns, Roe, & Ross, 1999). Thus, effective comprehension is also a constructive process.

Meaning constructed from the same text can vary greatly among readers because of their lack of knowledge or their inability to use their experiential backgrounds. By following a balanced approach to comprehension instruction, a teacher can ensure success for his or her students by planning either direct instruction or concept-development activities.

Strategy Instruction

Educators have spent many years searching for the best ways to teach reading comprehension. From this research, a multitude of proven strategies considered "best practices" have come forth. The object of this chapter is not to describe a variety of effective comprehension strategies. Rather, the intent is to motivate teachers to balance their comprehension instruction so that students acquire a repertoire of effective strategies to draw from when reading.

As with all instruction, balanced comprehension instruction requires that the classroom teacher assess his or her students' strengths and weaknesses; in this case, the teacher must assess students' abilities to flexibly use a variety of comprehension strategies based on their transactions with the text. Although all students need to be instructed in many different strategies for comprehending text, the teacher must determine particular strategies to concentrate on based on the needs of his or her students. For example, primary grade students are often comfortable making predictions and revising or confirming these predictions. However, these same students may not have solid strategies readily available to comprehend expository text. Balanced instruction provides students with a variety of comprehension strategies to choose from when reading.

In addition, teachers must strike a balance between whole-group comprehension instruction and developmentally appropriate comprehension instruction (Cooper, 1997). Whole-group instruction uses context and focuses on common strategies and skills from which all children can benefit. Instruction varies; a single strategy may be practiced several times or several strategies may be modeled. The teacher also balances various modes of reading—read-aloud, shared reading, guided reading, cooperative reading, or independent reading—ensuring that students receive the necessary support. Personal responses to and discussions about the reading indicate how well students are constructing meaning. Some students will require additional instructional support in particular strategies; for others, enrichment activities will be necessary.

All students need extension activities designed for application and development of reading skills.

Developmentally appropriate comprehension instruction follows the same model but incorporates some important differences. Several books at various levels are available to students, and the teacher chooses to read one text. Students then select their own text, perhaps choosing the one the teacher is reading, which offers the greatest amount of support. On a daily basis, students select their mode of reading with the understanding that they too must balance their choices. During discussions in literature circles composed of students reading the same text, the teacher attends to each group monitoring, supporting, and participating as needed. After students have personally responded to the text, the teacher supports different groups with individualized minilessons emphasizing the most effective comprehension strategies designed to meet the needs of the students in that group. Extension activities are then self-selected by the students.

Think-Aloud Strategy

Teachers who balance instruction not only tell, but they also show. Showing a student how something is done may be the best type of direct instruction available (Strickland, 1996). Because readers need to know that comprehension involves making connections between the topic and their knowledge, teachers can demonstrate how they comprehend a text in a think-aloud. A think-aloud is an instructional strategy that reveals a person's thinking; it literally is "thinking aloud." This strategy can be used very effectively to elucidate the connections students construct when reading, to assist students in understanding and developing their metacognitive skills, and to understand subtle symbolism, imagery, and foreshadowing in text. During the think-aloud process, the teacher makes his or her thinking public by modeling the activation of prior knowledge while reading a passage.

The Search for Delicious (Babbitt, 1969) is a developmentally appropriate text for students who are capable of reading beyond the expectations for fourth grade. After reading the beginning of this story, the teacher makes observations and begins to develop hypotheses and make predictions:

> The characters have strange names—DeCree, VaunGaylen, Hemlock. I know that a hemlock is a tree with poisonous berries or leaves. Why would the author give a character a name that means poison? Is she trying to tell me something about the character? Maybe I should look up the other names and see if they mean anything.

Thinking aloud encourages students to become conscious of the connections they are making between events in text or between the text and prior knowledge. Practice in identifying relationships and reasoning is essential to developing high-level thinking skills:

> The prologue explained how the only people who believed in dwarfs, woldwellers, and mermaids were children and the occasional worker of evil. This reminds me of the story Peter Pan because the adults don't believe in Never-Never Land, but the children do.

Think-alouds also can be used to demonstrate self-monitoring techniques and the application of "fix-up" strategies:

> Gaylen bit into an apple and found a nut inside. Why would the king give him an apple with a nut in it? That doesn't make sense. I read something about nuts before but I don't remember what it was. Let me go back and re-read until I find the passage.... Hemlock threw nuts at the dinner table. He put the nut in Gaylen's apple. That makes more sense because the king doesn't want to hurt Gaylen. Maybe the author is trying to show us that Hemlock is nuts—crazy.

The strength of the think-aloud is its versatility; it can be used to model a variety of strategies with all types of text, it forces students to examine their reading behaviors, and it promotes the development of higher level thinking skills.

Following are the steps in the think-aloud procedure adapted from Davey (1983):

Preparation—The teacher selects a short passage containing points of difficulty, ambiguities, or unknown words.

Modeling—The teacher reads the passage aloud as students follow along silently. The teacher stops and thinks through trouble spots orally and makes notations during demonstrations. He or she repeats modeling on several occasions.

Guided practice—Students work with partners to practice think-alouds. They take turns reading orally and sharing thoughts. Listening partners add thoughts after oral sharing is completed. Teachers choose different text types of varying lengths.

Independent practice—Students practice thinking through material silently. Teachers discuss how, when, and why the strategy works and most importantly how to modify the strategy.

Application—Teachers encourage students to think aloud while reading their assignments. This reading strategy helps students to think critically about the process of reading. It teaches students to become independent learners.

Reciprocal Teaching

Balanced reading instruction involves knowledge and critical reflection. Teachers must know about the reading process and the strategies that readers need in order to comprehend text (Iversen, 1994). Pressley (1998) writes that balanced comprehension instruction requires consistent, detailed monitoring of students as they read as well as detailed understanding of the reading tasks.

Teachers are expected to teach comprehension strategies to all the readers in their classrooms, providing opportunities for concept development and text understanding to occur. One technique developed to monitor comprehension is reciprocal teaching (Palincsar & Brown, 1984, 1986). Reciprocal teaching is a cooperative learning procedure in which students and teachers work together to improve students' understanding of complex texts and students' general ability to monitor their comprehension.

In a fourth-grade classroom, the text used for whole-group instruction might be a content area textbook, an anthology of stories, or a single novel such as *Maniac Magee* (Spinelli, 1990). A comprehension strategy from which the whole group can benefit, such as reciprocal teaching, is explored. Reciprocal teaching combines three strategies with which students are familiar (summarizing, questioning, and predicting) and one that encourages students to be aware of their metacognitive processes (clarifying). These four strategies are as follows:

Summarizing—Students summarize the most important elements of the text.

Questioning—Students ask questions after reading a segment of the text.

Clarifying—Students and teacher discuss reasons a portion of the text may be confusing because of difficult vocabulary of unfamiliar content. Teachers demonstrate appropriate repair strategies.

Predicting—Students predict the possible content of the text. The predictions are recorded.

Teacher modeling is essential for the success of reciprocal teaching because it incorporates several higher level thinking processes at once. For greatest success, students should become familiar with each of these processes alone before this strategy is introduced.

During the first lessons, the teacher models the process by summarizing the key points in her own words. The first few chapters of *Maniac Magee* might have the following summary:

> Jeffrey Magee's parents were killed in a train accident so he went to live with his aunt and uncle in the western part of Pennsylvania. His aunt and uncle hated each other and refused to share anything; this drove Jeffrey crazy. Jeffrey ran away from them because he couldn't take it anymore. He ran for a year and then ended up back in the eastern part of Pennsylvania where he was born. He met a few people in the town who were amazed by the things he could do such as Amanda, Hands Down, and the Pickwells. He earned the name "Maniac" by being able to perform incredible feats.

The question then posed to the group—How old was Jeffrey when he met Amanda?—may be answered directly from the text or may require the students to make inferences about the text; for example, What about Amanda drew Jeffrey to her?

After the question is answered to the satisfaction of the teacher, she clarifies a problem she had when reading the text and explains how she solved this problem. This part of the strategy is the most difficult for students to grasp because although they usually can ascertain their points of confusion, they often have trouble communicating their solutions. The prologue of *Maniac Magee* is confusing because it reveals events that will not occur until later in the book. A strategy that works well with this part of the text is to keep reading and see if the confusing sections are clarified by the text. The teacher might say,

> The first time I read this book, I had a lot of trouble understanding the prologue. It says that Maniac Magee was born in a dump, he runs all night, and he kissed a bull. When I read the first few chapters, I began to understand some of what that means. They say he was born in a dump because he is a homeless boy. They say he runs all night because he does run a great deal—he might have run across the state of Pennsylvania! But I do not understand the "kissed a bull" part. Because I figured out what the first two things meant by continuing to read, I will keep reading to see if my confusion is cleared up.

Clarifying a problem is not limited to comprehension; students also may choose to clarify how they decipher unknown words, such as reading to the end of the sentence, looking at the syllables, and substituting other words that make sense.

Finally, the teacher predicts what will happen next in the story. It is important for students to ground their predictions in text; the teacher must model this by stating the reasons why she predicts an event will occur.

> Because Maniac had to run away from the bullies at the baseball field, I predict that he will run to another town nearby or to another section of the town. He clearly cannot stay near Giant John McNab if he wants to stay in one piece.

Reciprocal teaching may have to be modeled several times before students can be expected to use this strategy independently. An excellent way to help students become comfortable with this method is to explore it during literature circles. In circles of four, each student is initially responsible for only one of the components: summarizing, questioning, clarifying, or predicting. During the next several sessions, students use different strategies until they have been responsible for all four. The teacher monitors these circles carefully so that she can support and guide students as they practice this technique. Any students having difficulty can be supported in individual conferences or in small-group lessons. When the students become comfortable using each of these strategies, they can take on the role of teacher—employing all four strategies as they teach the students in their literature circle. Each student has the opportunity to be the teacher.

As readers actively participate in the four steps of reciprocal teaching while working in small groups, the roles of teacher and students blend with increased student talk and reduced teacher talk. Students develop their ability to use these steps to construct meaning from a broad range of texts for a variety of purposes.

Metacognitive Awareness

As teachers make daily decisions about how to balance their reading instruction, they include opportunities for guided practice in their lessons. Teachers help their students determine how and when to apply strategies by showing readers how to monitor their comprehension.

Teachers know that proficient readers are careful in their reading and are aware of how well they understand what they read. Awareness is a key to being in control of comprehension. Successful readers also alter their reading strategies when portions of a text are not making sense. Metacognitive awareness means that readers are aware of what they do when they read, what to do when they encounter difficulties, and how to select strategies to accomplish their purposes for reading (Brown, 1985, as cited in Ruddell, 1999).

Figure 1
Comprehension Chart

MP	=	Making a Prediction
GVI	=	Got a Visual Image
RMO	=	Reminds Me Of
???	=	I'm Confused
RA	=	Read Again
SAT	=	Stop and Think
☺	=	No Sweat!

Adapted from Shanker, J.L., & Ekwall, E.E. (1998). *Locating and correcting reading difficulties* (7th ed.). Upper Saddle River, NJ: Merrill.

One of the most effective techniques to teach readers to monitor their thought processes when reading is to use a code for making reactions while reading passages (Shanker & Ekwall, 1998). Initially, the teacher selects an interesting passage at the readers' independent/instructional level. The teacher then explains that all readers process the same text in different ways, yet they can all comprehend it. During a small-group or large-group lesson, the teacher then models the techniques by marking the passage using a code similar to those shown in the comprehension chart in Figure 1. When readers are somewhat proficient in using the codes, paired reading is one way to continue independently.

Using Graphic Organizers as Aids to Comprehension

Another essential aspect of balancing comprehension instruction involves balancing the use and the teaching of narrative and expository text. The primary grades are overwhelmingly saturated with narrative stories. As a result, students tend to be familiar with story maps and story grammar. They can identify a story problem and resolution in the earliest grades. The scarcity of expository text written for the primary grades compared with the plethora of narrative stories available presents an additional obstacle to the teaching of expository text structure. In the intermediate grades, students are increasingly exposed to expository texts for which they often have no framework. Just as students must be taught the structure of narrative texts in order to internalize the essential elements of a story, students must be taught how to comprehend expository text.

Graphic organizers are invaluable tools for the teaching of expository text by spatially representing information. They provide a framework within which students can arrange the main ideas and supporting details, the sequence of events, and cause and effect.

Using the model for whole-group comprehension instruction discussed earlier, the teacher can use a content area textbook as the basis for whole-group instruction, reserving narrative text for developmentally appropriate instruction. In this way, a balance between the use of expository and narrative text is achieved. The benefits of using a content area textbook are considerable: instructional time increases, strategies for comprehending expository text are no longer neglected, and students learn content in context.

For example, a K-W-L chart (Ogle, 1986) (Figure 2) can be used easily to preview a chapter in a textbook. Students brainstorm what they already know about the subject in groups, as a class, or individually. These concepts are recorded in the first column *K*, for "What is *known*." Skimming the features of the textbook such as headings, graphics, and boldface print aids students' creation of questions for the second column *W*, for "What I *want* to know." In the final column *L*, "What I *learned*," students summarize key points covered in the text; the information in this column serves as a study guide for tests as well.

Many other graphic organizers elucidate the structure of expository text (see McGee & Richgels, 1985). Venn diagrams (see Figure 3 on page 48) compare and contrast key concepts and draw attention to similarities between concepts. Cause and effect maps (see Figure 4 on page 48) specifically delineate the sequence of events and can be used well with observing a scientific experiment over time or with tracking

Figure 2
K-W-L Chart

What I *know*	What I *want* to know	What I *learned*
• English settlers went to Virginia in search of gold but tobacco made the colony rich.	• What illnesses and hard times did the colonists have? • How did they save Jamestown?	• Salt water and mosquitos made the settlers sick. • The settlers didn't have the skills to survive. • The Virginia Company sent indentured servants to Jamestown.

Adapted from Ogle, D.M. (1986). K-W-L: A teaching model that develops active reading of expository text. *The Reading Teacher, 39*, 771–777.

episodes leading to a historical event. Detail maps (see Figure 5 on page 49) present a structure for determining main ideas and supporting details. Structured overviews (see Figure 6 on page 50) assist students with vocabulary and concept development as well as hierarchical relations between key concepts (Barron, 1969). There are a variety of excellent organizers available; however, the teacher must spend considerable time selecting appropriate graphic organizers to accommodate the needs of the students and the structure of the text. If there is not a balance between the graphic organizer, the students, and the text structure, students will not be able to internalize the framework necessary for comprehending expository text.

Figure 3
Venn Diagram

Charlie made his own cloak.
Charlie did everything himself.
Charlie was a shepherd.

red sheep berries seasons

Other people made the coat.
Momma and Anna traded for the things they needed for her coat.
Anna and Momma were poor.

Charlie Needs A Cloak

A New Coat For Anna

Figure 4
Cause and Effect Map

The Great Kapok Tree : A Tale of the Amazon Rain Forest

A man begins to chop down a great Kapok tree.

→ The insects explain that they pollinate the trees and flowers.

→ The monkeys explain that the tree roots keep the soil from washing away.

→ The birds explain that people burn the underbrush to clear the land.

The frogs explain that they will be homeless and hungry.

→ The porcupines explain that trees produce oxygen for animals and humans.

→ The sloth explains that the future world needs the beauty of the rain forest.

→ The man decides to leave the rain forest.

Adapted from McGee, L.M., & Richgels, D.J. (1985). Teaching expository text structure to elementary students. *The Reading Teacher, 38*, 739–748.

Figure 5
Detail Map for *Why Are Zebras Black and White?*

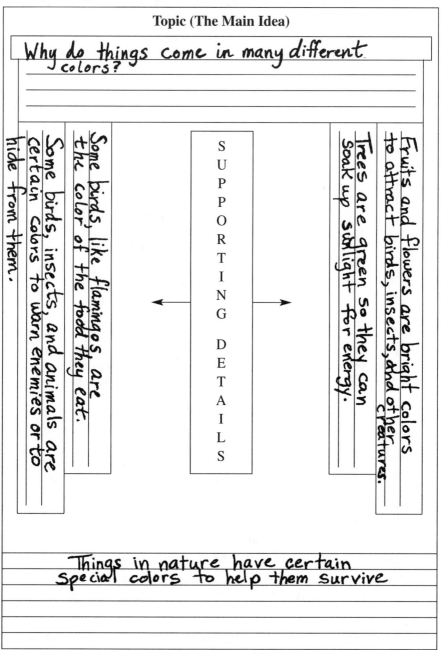

Topic (The Main Idea)

Why do things come in many different colors?

SUPPORTING DETAILS

Some birds, insects, and animals are certain colors to warn enemies or to hide from them.

Some birds, like flamingos are the color of the food they eat.

Fruits and flowers are bright colors to attract birds, insects, and other creatures.

Trees are green so they can soak up sunlight for energy.

Things in nature have certain special colors to help them survive

Figure 6
Structured Overview

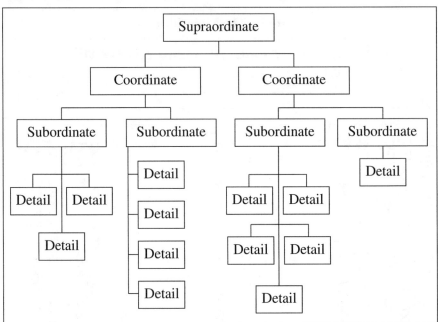

Adapted from Barron, R.R. (1969). Research for the classroom teacher: Recent developments on the structured overview as an advanced organizer. In H.L. Herber & J.D. Riley (Eds.), *Research in reading in the content areas: The first report* (pp. 28–47). Syracuse, NY: Syracuse University, Reading and Language Arts Center.

Final Thoughts

The teaching of comprehension is one of the most complex tasks for any teacher to undertake. The strategies described in this chapter are not new, yet when we consider several elements of balanced reading instruction, we can see their connection to this chapter.

One important aspect of balanced reading instruction that is congruent with these strategies is teacher decision making. Teachers are professionals who make choices about how to best meet the needs of their students. Their decision making involves what to teach (a poem or a word problem), who to teach (the whole class or a small group), when to teach (in the classroom or in the library), how to teach (reciprocal teaching or think aloud), and why to teach (which students need additional practice in applying comprehension strategies).

Another aspect of balanced reading instruction is materials. Many teachers use an abundance of materials to teach comprehension strategies. To teach the comprehension strategies outlined in this chapter, teachers can use both special reading materials such as teacher guides to a basal reader, or authentic texts such as trade books. For example, in teaching students how to read the directions of a science experiment, a teacher would rely on a science textbook or the accompanying laboratory workbook because the language of science experimentation is unique. However, to encourage students to recognize how science is a part of their daily lives, teachers will reprint articles from science magazines such as *Scientific American*. Again, the teachers' choice of materials is determined by their purpose, thus maintaining a balance in their teaching of the reading of scientific text.

Balanced reading instruction arises from knowledge and reflection. Iversen (1994) has written that teachers who know about the reading process will teach strategies within the context of a text. As described in this chapter, teachers scaffold instruction through teacher-led discussions during their daily lesson. As more research about literacy learning evolves, teachers will continue to reflect on, and thus refine, their teaching practices.

REFERENCES

Anderson, R.C., Hiebert, E.H., Scott, J.A., & Wilkinson, I.A.G. (1985). *Becoming a nation of readers: The report of the commission on reading*. Washington, DC: National Institute of Education.

Barron, R.R. (1969). Research for the classroom teacher: Recent developments on the structured overview as an advanced organizer. In H.L. Herber & J.D. Riley (Eds.), *Research in reading in the content areas: The first report* (pp. 28–47). Syracuse, NY: Syracuse University, Reading and Language Arts Center.

Burns, P.C., Roe, B.D., & Ross, E.P. (1999). *Teaching reading in today's elementary school* (7th ed.). Boston, MA: Houghton Mifflin.

Cooper, J.D. (1997). *Literacy: Helping children construct meaning* (3rd ed.). Boston, MA: Houghton Mifflin.

Davey, B. (1983). Think aloud—Modeling the cognitive processes of reading comprehension. *The Reading Teacher, 36*, 44–47.

Duffy, G.G., & Roehler, L.R. (1987). Teaching reading skills as strategies. *The Reading Teacher, 40*, 411–418.

Iversen, S. (1994). Balanced reading instruction: What children need to know and how to teach it. *Balanced Reading Instruction, 1*, 21–30.

McGee, L.M., & Richgels, D.J. (1985). Teaching expository text structure to elementary students. *The Reading Teacher, 38*, 739–748.

Ogle, D.M. (1986). K-W-L: A teaching model that develops active reading of expository text. *The Reading Teacher, 39*, 564–570.

Palincsar, A.S., & Brown, A.L. (1984). Reciprocal teaching of comprehension-fostering and comprehension-monitoring activities. *Cognition and Instruction, 2*, 117–175.

Palincsar, A.S., & Brown, A.L. (1986). Interactive teaching to promote independent learning from text. *The Reading Teacher, 39*, 771–777.

Pressley, M. (1998). *Reading instruction that works*. New York: Guilford.

Reutzel, D.R. (1998/1999). On balanced reading. *The Reading Teacher, 52*, 322–324.

Reutzel, D.R., & Cooter, R.B., Jr. (1999). *Balanced reading strategies and practices assessing and assisting readers with special needs*. Upper Saddle River, NJ: Merrill.

Ruddell, R.B. (1999). *Teaching children to read and write* (2nd ed.). Boston, MA: Allyn & Bacon.

Shanker, J.L., & Ekwall, E.E. (1998). *Locating and correcting reading difficulties* (7th ed.). Upper Saddle River, NJ: Merrill.

Spiegel, D.L. (1994). Finding the balance in literacy development for all children. *Balanced Reading Instruction, 1*, 6–11.

Spiegel, D.L. (1998). Silver bullets, babies, and bath water: Literature response groups in a balanced literacy program. *The Reading Teacher, 52*, 114–124.

Strickland, D.S. (1996, October/November). In search of balance: Restructuring our literary programs. *Reading Today*, p. 32.

CHILDREN'S LITERATURE REFERENCES

Babbitt, N. (1969). *The search for delicious*. New York: Farrar, Straus & Giroux.

Cherry, L. (1990). *The great Kapok tree: A tale of the Amazon rain forest*. San Diego, CA: Harcourt Brace Jovanovich.

DePaola, T. (1973). *Charlie needs a cloak*. New York: Simon and Schuster.

Martin, T. (1996). *Why are zebras black and white?* Boston, MA: Houghton Mifflin.

Spinelli, J. (1990). *Maniac Magee*. New York: HarperCollins.

Ziefert, H. (1986). *A new coat for Anna*. New York: Knopf.

CHAPTER 4

Literature in a Balanced Reading Program

Eileen M. Burke

In a balanced reading program, skills taught are perfected through stories—rich stories to which readers bond. In a balanced reading program, reading is skillful and richly satisfying because literature is of the highest quality and greatest variety. In its pursuit of literacy development, a balanced reading program is by definition committed to literature and to the skills that release its riches.

Purposes of Literature: A Constant

The purposes of literature remain constant no matter what the curriculum. Literature entertains; literature informs. During these processes, literary and cultural heritage is transmitted, imagination expands, and understanding of the human condition, of self and others, increases.

The call to story is powerful, and the hunger for more stories is insatiable. The call for fact is a rational need, and the hunger for information is infinite. Literature responds to both calls. The entertainment and information purposes of literature prosper in a balanced reading program.

Although the purposes of literature remain the same in every reading program, in a balanced reading program they are achieved by

- balancing what is known about child development and what is known about literacy development,
- balancing what is known about reading skills and what is known to be high quality literature,
- balancing and presenting all literary forms,
- balancing a range of reading with expectations about the depth of reading, and
- employing a range of literature extensions.

Balancing What Is Known About Child Development and What Is Known About Literacy Development

The rhythm, rhyme, and repetition in Mother Goose stories first introduced orally and later through picture storybooks start many young children's literacy adventures. From the well-known stories *This Is the House That Jack Built* (Adams, 1995) to *The Rose in My Garden* (Lobel, 1984) and onto *There Was an Old Lady Who Swallowed a Fly* (Taback, 1997), young children begin to stretch their auditory memories and then their visual awareness on cumulative verses while older children with ever-sharpening skills probe and understand the problems confronting the characters they meet. For example, older children recognize the loneliness of Leigh Botts in *Dear Mr. Henshaw* (Cleary, 1984), the dilemma of Catherine in *Catherine, Called Birdy* (Cushman, 1994), the survival strategies that Eily, Michael, and Peggy employ in *Under the Hawthorn Tree* (Conlon-McKenna, 1990), and the adoption of a mother in *Sarah, Plain and Tall* (MacLachlan, 1986).

Younger readers want to see how sounds look. *Chicken Soup With Rice* (Sendak, 1962) repeated on 12 calendar pages becomes familiar: The song and the book and the sight and the sound come together. Dr. Seuss satisfies children's desire for rhythm and chant. A balanced reading program offers both movement and words as in Marc Brown's

Rhyme series, the joy of word play in *17 Kings and 42 Elephants* (Mahy, 1987) and in *Jamberry* (Degen, 1983). Children seek more word fun after books like these. They will ask *Brown Bear, Brown Bear, What Do You See?* (Martin, 1967) and will sing the patterned speech in *Hush Little Baby* (Long, 1997). Much later, they will chortle at the title character's response to idioms in the Amelia Bedelia series (Parish) and plays on words as in *Agatha's Feather Bed* (Deedy, 1991).

Literature in the lives of young children nurtures their language development. Story-listening children *hear* new words. Children to whom adults read stories *hear* and *see* new words. Both sets of children are likely to use these new words. The play rhymes, rope chants, "A— My Name Is Alice" teasers are the oral introduction to the world of print. Children are fascinated with these words and with unusual ones like *didgeridoo* and *billibong goo* (Bogart, 1994), and words in tandem like *itsy bitsy* and words in groups like "hundreds of cats, thousands of cats, millions and billions and trillions of cats" (Gag, 1928). Children also love words they can sing:

Flies in the buttermilk,
Shoo, shoo, shoo
Flies in the buttermilk,
Shoo, shoo, shoo
Flies in the buttermilk,
Shoo, shoo, shoo

Skip to my Lou, my darling. (Quackenbush, 1975)

Children want to chant the taunt in *The Gingerbread Boy* (Galdone, 1979) and travel with the title character in *Miss Rumphius* (Cooney, 1992) and decide how to make the world more beautiful. They want to hear and to see the title character in *Goose* (Bangs, 1996) and learn about self-discovery, and produce the animal sounds of *Early Morning in the Barn* (Tafuri, 1983). In many barnyard stories such as *Barnyard Banter* (Fleming, 1994), children can play with barn sounds and giggle as they match sound with animal pictures and letters.

Literature fosters children's language development and strengthens their social, moral, emotional, and cognitive development. They ponder characters' actions and wonder how they might act in similar circumstances. They also feel for characters and their families, savor characters' courage, and rejoice in their self-discovery.

Later, children can grapple with the moral dilemma facing Marty in *Shiloh* (Naylor, 1991) and the struggle to survive facing Abel in *Abel's Island* (Steig, 1976). None of this happens, however, without the development of reading skills. Pleasure in reading increases as skills are strengthened.

Balancing What Is Known About Reading Skills and What Is Known to Be High-Quality Literature

As sound and sight symbols come together, convergent and divergent thinking are stimulated as are inferencing, hypothesizing, creating, empathizing, and vicarious emotional bonding. For young children, literary symbols and themes may be difficult to verbalize but young readers recognize the goodness and courage in a character's determination to keep a promise (for example, *Miss Rumphius*) and can sense and appreciate the theme before they can articulate it. In a story such as *The Gingerbread Boy*, readers can see the sad justice in the fate of the title character, whose arrogance is obvious, and begin to understand the function of the repetitive cumulative chant in the tale.

Through the problems and adventures of its characters and the excitement of its plots, literature serves child and human development in myriad ways. A balanced reading program assures that a rich variety of literature is made available, shared, discussed, and extended so that reading skills are nurtured on the best literature, and higher level thinking skills are challenged.

Immersion in many listening-to-literature experiences is likely to advance children's literacy development in many ways. According to

Carver and Leibert (1995), when students are engaged in listening to materials that are relatively difficult, that is, somewhat above their reading level, their vocabulary expands and their reading level improves. The listening experiences provide readers with a head start, or "bootstrap," toward literacy development.

Inferential thinking, deriving conclusions from evidence, can be nurtured by simple mystery stories and later challenged by such books as *The Mixed-Up Files of Mrs. Basil E. Frankweiler* (Konigsburg, 1967) and *The Giver* (Lowry, 1993).

Skillful readers can engage in linking the events of the plot in books like *The View From Saturday* (Konigsburg, 1996), in hypothesizing with Abel in *Abel's Island* (Steig, 1976), detecting subplots in *Walk Two Moons* (Creech, 1994), finding character foils in *Charlotte's Web* (White, 1952), identifying the relationship among the characters in *Of Nightingales That Weep* (Paterson, 1974), ferreting out the symbols in *The King's Fountain* (Alexander, 1971), and pondering the theme in *Missing May* (Rylant, 1992).

As the tools of word identification and meaning making are mastered, the reader seeks and engages in higher level thinking processes basic to the full appreciation of reading content. Without such tools, the achievement of deep reading and the excitement generated from it are not likely to develop and may be impossible to achieve.

Balancing and Presenting All Literary Forms

Beauty and diversity in the landscape of literature can generate fresh ideas in the minds of readers as balanced reading programs include a rich range of literature and a textbook-trade book blend that permeates the entire school day. No reading program stands isolated from the rest of the school curriculum.

In a balanced reading program, the forms and settings of literature are also in balance. Prose and poetry, fact and fiction, the present and the future, the present and the past, narration and illustration, exposition and narration, the traditional and the contemporary, the imaginative and the real—all genres and settings are presented and experienced. Because each literature type challenges comprehension and imagination in a somewhat different fashion, each offers a distinct pleasure and stimulation of its own. In a balanced reading program, each is incorporated and allowed to achieve its specific purposes.

Beginning Books

Beginning books include picture storybooks, wordless books, concept and counting books, alphabet and toy books, Mother Goose, and easy-to-read books that introduce the child to story and the world of print. These books also include point-and-say books in which the child sees familiar objects, identifies them, and notes how the names of the objects look in print.

Concept Books

Concept books help the young reader to focus on one major idea. High-quality concept books provide basic notions about core ideas such as size, shape, letters, numbers, colors, quantity, time, and place. Simple concept books such as alphabet and counting books give the young reader a sense of sequence, the basic tools of language and mathematics, and relevant and clear visuals to clarify the concepts.

Alphabet books

A, B, See (Hoban, 1982) challenges children to identify the many objects photographed that begin with the uppercase letter featured. *On Market Street* (Lobel, 1981) features vendors selling items that begin with the letters A to Z. Young readers can associate the object sold with the keyword and the key letter in this elegant point-and-say book. Like *On Market Street*, many alphabet books are themed; they are designed to transmit a great deal of information about the topic featured. Jerry Pallotta's alphabet book series represents well this type of concept book by presenting carefully researched scientific data organized around the alphabet.

Counting books

Counting books move the child forward and backward among the numerals. *Ten, Nine, Eight* (Bangs, 1983) is a subtraction story set in a young girl's bedroom. She is surrounded by toys, clothing, and stuffed animals that match the quantities featured. In *Moja Means One: Swahili Counting Book* (Feelings, 1972), the child sees the numerals from 1 to 10 and their sequence while learning about east African culture. In *One Grain of Rice: A Mathematical Folktale* (Demi, 1997), readers see how effectively and quickly one grain of rice, when doubled daily for 30 days, can greatly increase their resources. In *Seven Blind Mice* (Young, 1992), based on the well-known fable of *The Blind Man and the Elephant*, the author creates a counting book with powerful illustrations. Through brightly colored mice and one elephant, children learn colors, ordinal numbers, the days of the week, and the wisdom of not judging hastily.

Tana Hoban's *Shapes, Shapes, Shapes* (1970) and *Push-Pull, Empty-Full* (1972) focus on variation of form and on opposites. Gail Gibbons, Byron Barton, Bruce McMillan, and Donald Crews are authors and/or illustrators who have produced many excellent concept books for children. In a balanced reading program such books should be represented to support the development of major basic concepts.

Early Toy Books

Early toy books fascinate young children: They range from pop-ups, flap books, and "Venetian blind books," to cloth books, board books, plastic books, and die-cut covered books. Lifting flaps to find Spot seems perfectly sensible in *Where's Spot?* (Hill, 1980). *Look! Look! Look!* (Hoban, 1988) also makes sense to children. The reader looks at a square opening on a page that shows a small part of the colored photograph on the next page. Educated guesses are made and turning the page shows the object and solves the mystery. Children marvel when words and movable book parts match, as in *The Wheels on the Bus* (Zelinsky, 1990). Books with such features intrigue children and may provide a balance between the importance of toys and books in their development.

Mother Goose Books

Mother Goose stories prepare children in a unique fashion. They offer prose stories told in rhyme accented in strong rhythm. Literal, action filled, and very quick to resolution, Mother Goose characters are resilient and endearing. New editions continue to be published and lose none of the excitement in their repetition as *My Very First Mother Goose* (Opie, 1996) documents clearly.

Wordless Picture Books

Wordless picture books force children to tell about what they see and construct the story themselves. Getting the most information from pictures is a skill in need of full development. A balanced reading program's collection will include some titles helpful in developing picture-reading skill, in developing an understanding of the artist's craft, and in developing an appreciation for the marvels of narrative-visual blending. Children so instructed begin to grow in visual literacy—a prime skill because much of the information transmitted to children and adults is presented through illustrations.

High-Quality Picture Storybooks

High-quality picture storybooks are one of the best ways to help young children on the road to literacy. There is a continuous plot line they must follow, a picture responsible for transmitting part of the story message, and a collaboration between author and artist who together tell the story. Young children read between the lines and consider the partnership of picture and tale, learning much about the writing and picture craft while translating the story's message.

In *Officer Buckle and Gloria* (Rathmann, 1995) there is something about the way Officer Buckle looks, stands, walks, talks, prepares his presentations, and speaks that conveys his dedication and lack of confidence. There is also something about Gloria that shows her love for Mr. Buckle and her determination to carry his message. The artwork as well as the text convey the story's message.

In *The Old Dog* (Zolotow, 1995), the narrative portrays the sorrow and loneliness of the boy, Ben, who went to pat his dog in the morning and found she had died. The author tells the tale of Ben's grief well, but James Ransome's oil paintings register the gamut of Ben's feelings so the reader feels an intense emotional bond with the boy that would not be possible without the paintings.

Traditional Literature

Traditional literature includes the fables, folk tales, myths, legends, tall tales, and epics that transmit literary and cultural heritage. The motifs, common to many folk tales, the types of tales and their texts give evidence to the age and the range of the tales. The amazing number of forms of Cinderella, Little Red Riding Hood, and many others, seem to document a "world culture." Traditional literature is needed in all reading programs because of its universality but also because traditional literature helps support the multicultural understandings so important to human relationships worldwide.

The *fables* of old continue to teach new lessons. The busy ant and the lazy grasshopper herald the legacy of laziness; the clever fox and the vain crow will ever represent slyness and vanity; and the boy who cried "Wolf" teaches each of us to beware the search for unneeded attention. Fables are directly didactic—there are no apologies for the lessons they present. Children like them because the stories make their points clearly and bluntly.

At one time, *myths* offered explanations for natural phenomenon. Now they speak of supernatural beings and introduce readers to ancient societies, their beliefs, and their religions. The cast of gods and goddesses changes with each culture but there are strong similarities among all cultures. Children identify these similarities, examine the explanations of natural occurrences that are offered, and begin to understand and appreciate the symbolism in literature. *D'Aulaires' Book of Greek Myths*

(1962), *D'Aulaires' Norse Gods and Giants* (1986), *The Olympians* (Fisher, 1984), *In the Beginning: Creation Stories From Around the World* (Hamilton, 1988), and *Goddesses, Heroes, and Shamans: The Young People's Guide to World Mythology* (Bellingham, 1994) suggest that although the myths are ancient, they are alive and well in the 20th century.

To bring myths into modern times, Jane Yolen and other modern myth writers have taken the characteristics of myths and woven them into books such as *The Girl Who Cried Flowers* (1974) and *The Faery Flag: Stories and Poems of Fantasy and the Supernatural* (1989). The myth's form is constantly re-presented in narrative adaptations and in rich illustration, as is the case with *Beowulf* (Crossley-Holland, 1982). This epic is told in narrative form and is extensively illustrated.

The heroes—real and exaggerated—in *legends* and *tall tales* intrigue children. Because legends have, by definition, some root in history, they belong in the school's overall curriculum as well as in its reading program. Characters such as King Arthur, Robin Hood, the Knights of the Round Table, St. George, and William Tell should be invited into classrooms; they represent a time and place lost to children today unless they are shared through literature. Tall tale heroes such as Pecos Bill and Paul Bunyan offer readers not only enjoyment and cultural history, but they introduce young readers to the fun of hyperbole.

In a balanced reading program, traditional literature's links to the present time will be rediscovered and fresh applications of their symbolism found. Folk tales from around the world should permeate not only reading activities but also the social studies curriculum. The Anansi tales from Africa, the Jack tales from Britain, the French folk tales and fairy tales, tales from the Arabian Nights, and Native American tribal tales can help children understand a world larger than their own.

Modern Fantasy

Modern fantasy demands the reader's attention; the suspension of disbelief while reading the story is maintained only by the writer's consistency in creating the fantasy. To document such consistency requires careful reading of the text. Tolkien and Alexander are true to the worlds they create, that is, every detail of the fantasy is consistent with the fantasy world itself. There are no contradictions; the fantasy world is all of one piece and appears very real.

The Narnia tales (Lewis) and *The Giver* (Lowry, 1993) provoke questions about power, and *Tuck Everlasting* (Babbitt, 1975) stirs questions about immortality. The whole notion of these "what-would-happen-if" tales sends the imagination soaring.

Poetry

If tales from around the world should permeate the reading and social studies curriculum, poetry should flavor the entire school day. There is no genre equal to poetry in weaving word music and word magic. Rhythm, rhyme, repetition, imagery, and figurative language are the poet's tools. Shel Silverstein's humor, Jack Prelutsky's and Eve Merriam's word play, Valerie Worth's succinctness, Myra Cohn Livingston's craftsmanship, Deborah Chandra's imagery, Barbara Esbensen's powerful word pictures, Lear's nonsense, and Dickinson's profoundness should be sampled by every child. In addition to the content of poems, much can be learned from poetry sharing about the poet's tools and how to use them, about the wisdom of conciseness, and about the impact of image. Themed anthologies abound and such collections as *Hand in Hand* (Hopkins, 1994) bring together periods of history, poetry and illustration.

Contemporary Realism

Contemporary realism is a popular genre. It offers young readers plots relevant to their lives. It offers the readers characters who confront problems they recognize or can easily imagine they might face. Because these tales present real-life events, they are most discussible and debatable. Activities such as book read, book think, and book talk are especially appropriate here. Skilled writers such as Lloyd Alexander, Avi,

Betsy Byars, Beverly Cleary, Robert Cormier, Karen Cushman, Paula Fox, Jean Craighead George, Katherine Paterson, Gary Paulsen, Richard Peck, and Cynthia Voigt offer characters and plots that grip attention and beg to be discussed. The content of these books and the reader's relationship to the problems and events elevate the discussion to a high level of vicarious experiencing, so linking literature to the lives of readers is accomplished most easily with this genre.

Historical Fiction

It is a small wonder that historical fiction is well represented in the list of Newbery medal books. The research basic to presenting accurately another era and setting requires skill, perseverance, and imagination. In addition to meeting high-quality writing standards, authors of historical fiction must present characters who are credible. Patricia Beatty, Patricia Clapp, Alice Dalgliesh, Marguerite DeAngeli, Paul Fleischman, Jean Fritz, Virginia Hamilton, Kathryn Lasky, Lois Lowry, Scott O'Dell, Elizabeth George Speare, Rosemary Sutcliff, Mildred Taylor, and Laura Ingalls Wilder write fiction rooted solidly in fact that transforms readers into characters from years past. In each individual's march to wider arenas of understanding, it may be as important to understand other times as it is to understand other cultures.

Multicultural Literature

Multicultural literature is literature that helps readers understand, acknowledge, and respect one another's cultural roots. It focuses on racial, ethnic, and religious minorities; on regional cultures; and on the disabled and elderly. Because it represents such a wide area of focus, it is represented in many genres, particularly traditional literature, historical fiction, contemporary realistic fiction, and nonfiction.

Ethnic diversity in the United States seems limitless. Here, multicultural literature is often used to mean the literature of African Americans, Native Americans, Hispanic Americans, and Asian Americans. A principal goal in multicultural literature is that, in presenting minorities, stereotypes are rejected and individuals emerge. Taking pains to use literature that is authentic folklore can help to assure an accurate presentation of cultures. Verna Aardema, Arnold Adoff, Ashley Bryan, Eloise Greenfield, Virginia Hamilton, Mary Lyons, and Patricia and Frederick McKissack are among many writers who speak with a strong voice of African American roots and history.

Native American tales range widely. Many tribes with tales unique to them enrich genre collections. There are traditional and trickster tales, creation tales, and fictional tales about many tribes, for example, Byrd Baylor's poetic writing of the Southwestern desert (1975), Paul Goble's tales of the Indians of the Great Plains, *The Ghost Horse Cycle* (Highwater, 1984), *The Sign of the Beaver* (Speare, 1983), *Sing Down the Moon* (O'Dell, 1970), *Sweetgrass* (Hudson, 1984), and *Annie and the Old One* (Miles, 1971).

Hispanic American literature includes a great variety of settings, cultures, and time periods. Books like *The Hispanic Americans* (Meltzer, 1982) detail the influence of Hispanic culture on the United States. Others like *The Honorable Prison* (Jenkins, 1989) speak to the political unrest in parts of Latin America and the effect on families.

Hispanic American literature is well represented in *Once in Puerto Rico* (Belpre, 1973), *Moon Tired of Walking on Air* (Belting, 1992), tales from the Indians of South America, John Bierhorst's many Aztec tales, *Secret of the Andes* (Clark, 1952), *El Bronx Remembered* (Mohr, 1986), Scott O'Dell's Mayan tales, and Gary Soto's Mexican American stories. Together these tales represent a great range of Hispanic literature that balances the traditional and current and spans the huge area from Puerto Rico and Mexico to South America and from the New York City of today to the Aztec, Incan, and Mayan cultures of yesterday.

Asian American literature also is represented in many genres and streams from many cultures and political views. *Many Lands, Many Stories: Asian Folktales for Children* (Conger, 1987) includes tales from many Asian countries. The range of Asian American literature, as with much culturally based literature, bridges the humorous and the serious. *How My Parents Learned to Eat* (Friedman, 1984) is quite different in tone from *The Year of the Impossible Goodbyes* (Choi, 1991), a tale of a Korean family's troubled experiences during the many occupations of Korea. Picture books like *Grandfather's Journey* (Say, 1993), *Tree of Cranes* (Say, 1991), and *Angel Child, Dragon Child* (Surat, 1983) say much in narration and illustration to young children about Asian culture. The Chinese American tales of Laurence Yep speak to the differences and similarities of these two cultures.

Biography and Information Books
Biography

Children are ready to worship heroes and heroines. Biographies illustrating journeys to achievement of people in all types of careers are a gift to children through which they can stretch their own horizons. A Very Young Series (Krementz, 1977) and biographies like *Lou Gehrig: The Luckiest Man* (Adler, 1997) introduce young readers to the effort and discipline that high-quality work demands. Acquaintance with prominent figures in many fields alerts young readers to the options they have and widens their understanding of the scope of talents needed in the world.

From the simple, brief biographies of Peter Tchaikovsky (Venezia, 1994), Aaron Copeland (Venezia, 1995), and Phillis Wheatley (Greene, 1995), to the beautifully illustrated biography of Rosa Bonheur (Turner, 1991), to the well-documented biographies of Abraham Lincoln (Freedman, 1987) and Eleanor Roosevelt (Freedman, 1993), a great range of fascinating and accurate accounts of historical figures are available for children.

Information books

Nonfiction books are focal and vital in this age of information. Due to sophisticated technology in photography and illustration, texts offer facts with clarity, beauty, and accuracy. There seems to be no topic that is unexamined. Fact and fiction are often presented together in books where tale or fable and fact share the pages. Sometimes genres are mixed as in the Magic School Bus books (Cole) and Tomie dePaola's

The Cloud Book (1975) and *The Popcorn Book* (1978). Sometimes fact is presented starkly with stunning photography as in *Storms* (Simon, 1992), or with detailed, precise drawings as in Macaulay's *Castle* (1978), *Cathedral* (1973), *Mill* (1983), and *Ship* (1993).

Balancing a Range of Reading With Expectations About the Depth of Reading

Readers in a balanced reading program will experience both broad and deep reading. The breadth of all literature types, as noted in the previous section, makes broad reading possible. When literature itself provokes thought and reflection through profound themes, characters challenged by problems, and plots linked by events that are held together by an appealing style, then readers can engage in deep reading.

Some works that demand and provoke deep reading and profound thinking follow. The core events and problems in these books stimulate reflection; they address the deep, basic problems of the human condition—problems that are always current. Many of these problems are visible in recent newspaper headlines. Skillful readers will be challenged by these books.

In *Shiloh* (Naylor, 1991), Marty confronts a legal-versus-ethical dilemma. Should he keep, nourish, and protect Shiloh, an abused beagle, or should he return the dog to the owner who is guilty of the abuse?

The title character in *Lyddie* (Paterson, 1991) tries to keep her family together but is confronted by poverty, abandonment, intimidation, and an ineffective mother.

The title character in *Catherine Called Birdy* (Cushman, 1994), living in the Middle Ages, fights to prevent her father from forcing her to marry against her will. In *Shabanu* (Staples, 1989), the title character in a totally different time and place fights for the right to refuse the life partner chosen for her, but cultural mores are strongly against her.

Leigh Botts in *Dear Mr. Henshaw* (Cleary, 1984) fights loneliness caused by his parents' separation.

Weighty problems such as freedom of choice face Jonas in *The Giver* (Lowry, 1994). In *Number the Stars* (Lowry, 1990), Annmarie is called to bravery. In *Tuck Everlasting* (Babbit, 1975), Winnie Foster faces the choice of mortality or immortality.

These works and their authors challenge skillful readers to probe areas that often baffle adults. Engaging skillful readers in deep reading and deep thinking stimulates and engrosses them. Teachers who provide a reading program that balances pleasurable offerings with the skill building needed to savor that pleasure serve their students well.

Employing a Range of Literature Extensions

Prereading and postreading activities in a balanced reading program ought to engage the full talents of the reader. Book talk should be preceded by "book think" and should follow high-quality literature. It is often in the post-book talk that readers come to appreciate the depth and range of the author's plot, the skill in contriving it, the depth of characters, and the interplay of plot with characters and characters with characters.

In balanced reading programs, teachers engage readers in post-book discussions in which themes are identified and healthy debate occurs. Presenting views and arguing points challenges skillful readers and forces a careful reflection of what they have read before they speak.

The extensions of some books seem to invite writing; other books lead to art extension, crafts, prolonged reflection, or research. Perhaps the measure of a high-quality book is that it does demand reflection; it does provoke review. It says, "Pay attention to me. Think about what I am saying." The subsequent response will depend not only on the text but on the reader's interest and skill.

Whatever the extension, it ought to bring the book into the life of the reader; into an arena of everyday living or fantasizing that contributes to the reader's full development in many ways. Literature contributes to language expansion, of course, but also to a cognitive stretch, a creative period, a transformation from narrative to the visual, a dialogue of measured thought, a grappling with emotions, an understanding of the motivations of the characters, and a recognition of the advancement of science, mathematics, art, or medicine. It is never too early to provoke book-living links. Such links are best forged when prereading activities prepare the reader for a unique experience and postreading activities extend and deepen the intensity of that experience.

REFERENCE

Carver, R.P., & Leibert, R.E. (1995). The effect of reading library books at different levels of difficulty upon gain in reading ability. *Reading Research Quarterly, 30*, 46.

CHILDREN'S LITERATURE REFERENCES

Adams, P. (1995). *This is the house that Jack built*. Rochester Hills, MI: Childs Play.

Adler, D. (1997). *Lou Gehrig: The luckiest man*. Ill. T. Widener. North Bay, ON: Gulliver Books.

Alexander, L. (1971). *The king's fountain*. Ill. E.J. Keats. New York: Dutton.

Babbitt, N. (1975). *Tuck everlasting*. New York: Farrar.

Bangs, M. (1983). *Ten, nine, eight*. New York: Viking.

Bangs, M. (1996). *Goose*. New York: Scholastic.

Baylor, B. (1975). *The desert is theirs*. New York: Scribner.

Bellingham, D. (1994). *Goddesses, heroes, and shamans: The young people's guide to world mythology*. New York: Kingfisher.

Belpre, P. (1973). *Once in Puerto Rico*. Ill. C. Price. New York: Warner.

Belting, N. (1992). *Moon tired of walking on air*. Ill. Will Hillenbrand. Boston, MA: Houghton.

Bogart, J.E. (1994). *Gifts*. Ill. B. Reid. New York: Scholastic.

Brown, M. (1988). *Party rhymes*. New York: Penguin.

Choi, S.N. (1991). *The year of the impossible goodbyes*. New York: Dell.

Clark, A. (1952). *Secret of the Andes*. Ill. J. Charlot. New York: Viking.

Cleary, B. (1984). *Dear Mr. Henshaw*. New York: Dell.

Cole, J. Magic school bus series. Ill. B. Degan. New York: Scholastic.

Conger, D. (1987). *Many lands, many stories: Asian folktales for children*. Ill. R. Ra. Boston, MA: Tuttle.

Conlon-McKenna, M. (1990). *Under the Hawthorn tree*. Dublin, Ireland: O'Brien Press.

Cooney, B. (1992). *Miss Rumphius*. New York: Viking.

Creech, S. (1994). *Walk two moons*. New York: HarperCollins.

Crossley-Holland, K. (1982). *Beowulf*. New York: Oxford University Press.

Cushman, K. (1994). *Catherine, called Birdy*. Boston, MA: Houghton.

D'Aulaire, I., & D'Aulaire, E.P. (1962). *D'Aulaires' book of Greek myths*. New York: Doubleday.

D'Aulaire, I., & D'Aulaire, E.P. (1967). *D'Aulaires' Norse gods and giants*. New York: Doubleday.

Deedy, C.A. (1991). *Agatha's feather bed*. Ill. L.L. Seeley. Atlanta, GA: Peachtree.

Degen, B. (1983). *Jamberry*. New York: Harper & Row.

Demi. (1997). *One grain of rice: A mathematical folktale*. New York: Scholastic.

dePaola, T. (1975). *The cloud book*. New York: Holiday.

dePaola, T. (1978). *The popcorn book*. New York: Holiday.

Feelings, M. (1992). *Moja means one: Swahili counting book*. Ill. T. Feelings. New York: Dial.

Fisher, L.E. (1984). *The Olympians: Great gods and goddesses of ancient Greece*. New York: Holiday.

Fleming, D. (1994). *Barnyard banter*. New York: Henry Holt.

Freedman, R. (1989). *Lincoln: A photobiography*. New York: Clarion.

Freedman, R. (1993). *Eleanor Roosevelt*. New York: Clarion.

Friedman, I.R. (1984). *How my parents learned to eat*. Ill. A. Say. Boston, MA: Houghton.

Gag, W. (1928). *Millions of cats*. New York: Putnam.

Galdone, P. (1979). *The gingerbread boy*. New York: Clarion.

Goble, P. (1978). *The girl who loved wild horses*. New York: Bradbury.

Greene, C. (1995). *Phillis Wheatley: First African-American poet*. Chicago, IL: Children's Press.

Hamilton, V. (1988). *In the beginning: Creation stories from around the world*. Ill. B. Moser. Orlando, FL: Harcourt Brace Jovanovich.

Highwater, J. (1997). *The ghost horse cycle*. Bridgewater, NJ: Replica.

Hill, E. (1980). *Where's Spot?* New York: Viking.

Hoban, T. (1970). *Shapes, shapes, shapes*. New York: Greenwillow.

Hoban, T. (1972). *Push-pull, empty-full*. New York: Macmillan.

Hoban, T. (1982). *A, B, See!* New York: Greenwillow.

Hoban, T. (1988). *Look! Look! Look!* New York: Greenwillow.

Hopkins, L.B. (1994). *Hand in hand*. Ill. P.M. Fiore. New York: Simon & Schuster.

Hudson, J. (1984). *Sweetgrass*. New York: Scholastic.

Jenkins, L.B. de (1989). *The honorable prison*. New York: Lodestar.

Konigsburg, E.L. (1967). *The mixed-up files of Mrs. Basil E. Frankweiler*. New York: Atheneum.

Konigsburg, E.L. (1996). *The view from Saturday*. New York: Atheneum.

Krementz, J. A very young series. New York: Knopf.

Lewis, C.S. The Narnia series. New York: Macmillan.

Lobel, A. (1981). *On Market Street*. Ill. A. Lobel. New York: Morrow.

Lobel, A. (1984). *The rose in my garden*. Ill. A. Lobel. New York: Morrow.

Long, S. (1997). *Hush little baby*. San Francisco, CA: Chronicle.

Lowry, L. (1990). *Number the stars*. Boston, MA: Houghton.

Lowry, L. (1993). *The giver*. Boston, MA: Houghton.

Macauley, D. (1973). *Cathedral*. Boston, MA: Houghton.

Macauley, D. (1978). *Castle*. Boston, MA: Houghton.

Macauley, D. (1983). *Mill*. Boston, MA: Houghton.

Macauley, D. (1993). *Ship*. Boston, MA: Houghton.

MacLachlan, P. (1986). *Sarah, plain and tall*. New York: Harper.

Mahy, M. (1987). *17 kings and 42 elephants*. Ill. P. MacCarthy. New York: Dial.

Martin, B. Jr. (1967). *Brown bear, brown bear, what do you see?* Ill. E. Carle. New York: Henry Holt.

Meltzer, M. (1982). *The Hispanic Americans*. New York: Crowell.

Miles, M. (1971). *Annie and the old one*. Ill. P. Parnell. Boston, MA: Little, Brown

Mohr, N. (1986). *El Bronx remembered*. Houston, TX: Arte Publico.

Murphy, J. (1988). *The last dinosaur*. New York: Scholastic.

Naylor, P. (1991). *Shiloh*. New York: Dell.

O'Dell, S. (1970). *Sing down the moon*. New York: Dell.

Opie, I. (1996). *My very first Mother Goose*. Ill. by R. Wells. Cambridge, MA: Candlewick.

Parish, P. Amelia Bedelia series. New York: HarperCollins.

Paterson, K. (1974). *Of nightingales that weep*. New York: Harper.

Paterson, K. (1991). *Lyddie*. New York: Viking.

Quackenbush, R. (1975). *Skip to my Lou*. Philadelphia, PA: Lippincott.

Rathmann, P. (1995). *Officer Buckle and Gloria*. New York: Putnam.

Rylant, C. (1992). *Missing May*. Danbury, CT: Orchard.

Say, A. (1993). *Grandfather's journey*. Boston, MA: Houghton.

Say, A. (1991). *Tree of cranes*. Boston, MA: Houghton.

Sendak, M. (1962). *Chicken soup with rice*. New York: HarperCollins.

Simon, S. (1992). *Storms*. New York: Morrow.

Speare, E.G. (1983). *The sign of the beaver*. New York: Dell

Staples, S.F. (1989). *Shabanu: Daughter of the wind*. New York: Knopf.

Steig, W. (1976). *Abel's Island*. New York: Farrar.

Surat, M.M. (1983). *Angel child, dragon child*. Ill. V. Mai. Austin, TX: Raintree.

Taback, S. (1997). *There was an old lady who swallowed a fly*. New York: Viking.

Tafuri, N. (1983). *Early morning in the barn*. New York: Greenwillow.

Turner, R.M. (1991). *Rosa Bonheur*. Boston, MA: Little Brown.

Venezia, M. (1994). *Peter Tchaikovsky*. Chicago, IL: Children's Press.

Venezia, M. (1995). *Aaron Copeland*. Chicago, IL: Children's Press.

White, E.B. (1952). *Charlotte's web*. New York: Harper.

Yolen, J. (1989). *The faery flag: Stories and poems of fantasy and the supernatural*. New York: Orchard.

Yolen, J. (1976). *The girl who cried flowers*. Ill. D. Palladini. New York: Crowell.

Young, E. (1992). *Seven blind mice*. New York: Putnam.

Zelinsky, P. (1990). *The wheels on the bus*. New York: Dutton.

Zolotow, C. (1995). *The old dog*. Ill. J. Ransome. New York: Harper.

CHAPTER 5

Assessing Literacy Learners: A Tale of Two Children

Delores E. Heiden

A ssessment is a critically important responsibility and challenge in any teacher's work with children and their developing literacy skills and abilities. To really understand what instruction our students need, we must continually assess how much they know and what they can do. As Dixie Lee Spiegel points out in Chapter 1, research shows clearly that although most instructional approaches work for some children, there is no one single approach that works for every child. As all the contributors to this book emphasize, a balanced approach to literacy instruction requires that teachers select the most appropriate types of instruction based on what they know about the children they teach. This balance can be achieved only if teachers know a great deal about their students through careful observation and skillful assessment of the students' knowledge and abilities as readers and writers.

The focus of this chapter is on assessment for the purpose of informing instruction in reading at the elementary level. The assessments treated in this chapter all originate from a single, all-important question: What do teachers need to know about children so that we can best support their growth and learning? The basic guidelines to developing an assessment program are start small, keep it simple, and do not discard what already works. The overarching message is that teachers must know each child in their classrooms, and that a solid assessment program is essential in a balanced literacy program; good assessment is absolutely necessary to inform instruction so we can move children to where they need to go next.

We will begin this chapter by getting to know two children, Tyler and Andrew (pseudonyms). The children live in a small city in the midwestern United States and go to a school in a relatively traditional setting. Their literacy skills, habits, attitudes, and interests are not unlike those of most elementary-age children throughout the United States. Through the discovery of what these two children know, can do, and choose to do as readers, we may consider the possible ways such discoveries can be made about other children in other classrooms. We will look at both Tyler's and Andrew's reading and writing capabilities and the assessment tools that might be used to reveal who these children are as literacy learners.

Tyler and Andrew: A First Look

Tyler is in first grade, and Andrew is in fourth grade. Although these children both are in elementary school, they are at very different places in their development as readers and writers. What do their teachers need to know about Tyler and Andrew to be able to effectively support their progress as learners? In this chapter we will look at the results of assessments that were done with these children across the school year, including some observations made at the start of the year, ongoing assessments made during the year, and observations made at the end of the year. Although there are important differences in the type of information their teachers want to have about the reading and writing skills and abilities these two children possess, there are some common features in the ways in which their teachers will gather the information they need to assess and evaluate the children's progress.

Tyler

Tyler is very independent but wants to be liked by the other boys in his class. Although Tyler really wants to be accepted by his classmates, he does not always know how to go about interacting with them, and sometimes he behaves inappropriately. At times, his willfulness has gotten him into trouble on the playground. He can stretch his teacher's patience to the limit and then present her with an apple or a picture he has colored. Tyler likes animals, the Chicago Bulls, and hunting. He greatly admires his stepfather, who is an avid hunter, and Tyler can tell all about the proper equipment needed for hunting deer or duck. Tyler likes to fantasize about himself as a hunter. He also likes to tell stories that may or may not be true. When he experiences problems at school, Tyler will say that he is moving away tomorrow and he will not be back. Things have been difficult at school for Tyler; he started his first-grade year at the bottom of his class, a class that his teacher reports is, overall, one of the highest achieving first-grade groups she has had in recent years. Tyler's mother is very concerned that he learns how to read in first grade, and she works with him every night at home.

Andrew

Andrew is a worrier, procrastinator, and divergent thinker; a person with a well-developed sense of humor; a child who blames himself for all of life's catastrophes and minor annoyances; an occasional reader and writer; and a person who sincerely wants to do well, and often does. Ask him about his favorite subject in fourth grade and he will say it is recess. He is the boy by the window who looks outside to daydream, and he is the one whose desk eats his assignments and spits out the papers, books, and pencil stubs that lie in disarray around his feet. This is the child whom every teacher will recognize as the one who is quite capable but somehow misses the mark due to his lack of organization. Every other child's paper has been handed in and they have all gone to recess, but Andrew is at his desk redoing an assignment because he cannot find the first one that he had done at home the night before. Start a conversation about some topic in science or social studies, and you will not be able to get in a word edgewise. Take a look at standardized test results, and you will see that Andrew falls in the above-average range in every school subject, except math, for which he is in the average range. His report cards are inconsistent, but generally Andrew brings home grades in the A-/B+ range.

To get a good profile of Tyler and Andrew, we can glean information from a variety of sources: classroom observation, daily work, tests, standardized assessments, informal assessments, and conversations with the children and their parents. Although the things we need to assess are very different for two children at such very different stages in their development as readers and writers, the assessment techniques we employ may be very similar. Given that a balanced approach must be built on a comprehensive view of literacy, we need to gather information about individual children across a wide spectrum, including word identification, construction of meaning, reading attitudes, habits and interests, and writing. A balanced approach requires teachers to be decision makers. Teachers can only be thoughtful decision makers if they understand where their students are as literacy learners. The key is to create a systematic approach to gathering information, and to use it on a regular basis to help stay abreast of how children are developing as readers and writers.

Assessing Tyler's Literacy Skills

Tyler entered first grade having already experienced failure as a learner; he even repeated kindergarten. Although he has a great deal of awareness of the world around him and is confident in the ways in which he handles himself and relates to others, Tyler also had a number of behaviors that got in the way of his learning. His mother was very concerned about Tyler's development as a reader; she asked his teacher to arrange for extra help in reading for him in his first month of first grade. Her fears were justified as Tyler struggled with reading and writing from the start. Following are some powerful assessment tools that can tell us what Tyler knew about print at the beginning of Grade 1.

Concepts About Print

Marie Clay's concepts about print (CAP) test (1993) is an invaluable tool for assessing children's knowledge about print and its functions. At the start of the school year, Tyler had a good sense of directionality and book handling. He knew that print contains a message, and he knew where to start and which way to go when reading on a page. The CAP test also indicated that Tyler did not yet have a clear concept of the differences between letter and word and was not yet ready to match voice to print successfully. He was not yet attending to print and was unable to pick up on the anomalies in word or letter order; instead he looked to the pictures to find clues. He was not yet aware of punctuation. Tyler quickly grew disinterested in the tasks required of him in the CAP test. He was concerned about his performance, however; he repeatedly asked to know what responses his friend gave to particular items when the other boy was given the same test.

Letter Identification

Not unlike a number of children in almost every first-grade class at the start of the school year, Tyler was at an emergent level in reading development, typified by his reliance on picture cues to read stories (Leslie & Jett-Simpson, 1997). When Tyler was presented with letter identification tasks, it was discovered that his knowledge of letter-sound relations was not yet complete; *H* eluded him and he identified both *V* and *Q* as *U*. He did know the sounds for all letters except for *F*, *H*, *U*, and *L*, for which he used the sound "eh." Tyler could generate words for all the letters except *V* and *Y*, relying heavily on his strong knowledge of letters at the beginning of other children's names. This began to give the examiner a hint of Tyler's rather considerable visual memory.

Writing

Requests for his writing caused Tyler frustration at the start of the year; he was not sure what was expected of him and he was not sure that those letters and sounds he knew actually connected with words

---

that could be written on paper. When asked to write all the words he knew on Clay's writing vocabulary assessment (1993), Tyler was able to produce the numeral 2 for the word *to* and write his own name. However, he was aware of print around the room and copied strings of letters onto his paper. Although these were obviously without any meaning for him, Tyler was aware that the print around him might be used to fulfill the task he had been given.

For Clay's dictation test (1993), Tyler was asked to write the following dictated sentences: "I have a big dog at home. Today I am going to take him to school." Tyler was able to produce, *I H N B D O G AT 2 A I M D 2 C . 2*. His writing indicates that Tyler could hear and record letters for a number of phonemes in the sentences. In several instances, Tyler used single letters to represent whole words, although he was able to write the words *I*, *dog*, and *at*. His mix of letters and numerals suggests that he is not yet distinguishing between the two. Based on this dictation sample and other samples of his writing at the time, Tyler appeared to be at a phonemic or early letter-name stage in spelling development (Ferreiro, 1986).

Teacher Observations

Another critical tool is the set of observations made by his teacher about how Tyler was able to function as a reader within the classroom. Tyler enjoyed listening to stories, sat quietly and followed the storyline, and interacted with the rest of the children at appropriate places. He spontaneously retold portions of the story later, and he displayed his interest in having others read to him.

Running Records

Tyler was enrolled in an early-intervention program (Jett-Simpson & Greenewald, 1996) in the fall of his first-grade year. As he gained understanding of reading strategies and began to read simple stories, running records (Clay, 1993; Johnston, 1997) proved to be an invaluable tool to help his teacher decide when and how to accelerate his progress. By midyear, Tyler was using a number of word-identification strategies effectively. Figure 1 is an example of a running record taken during Tyler's reading of the book, *Yes, Ma'am* (Melser, 1985).

The running record shown in Figure 1 represents just over half the book that Tyler read. To save space, not all of the record is reproduced here, but the record shown is representative of Tyler's reading of the entire book. We can see that Tyler is consistent throughout when he drops the *-it* phonogram or "chunk" in the nonsense word *sloppity* (and does the same later in the text with *glumpity* and *buckity*). He is able to monitor his own reading and self-correct at a couple of points with a fair degree of success; he self-corrects about a third of his miscues in the reading of the whole book. Overall, his reading falls in the instructional range from 90%–94% accuracy. Clearly, this book is a good match for him at this stage in his reading development.

Running records can tell us a great deal more than just the match between child and text, however. They are an invaluable tool for helping teachers observe exactly which types of miscues children are making, and how children are attempting to make use of the interactive cue systems (for example, graphic, syntactic, semantic, visual) in word identification (Clay, 1994). The running records helped Tyler's teacher analyze his specific reading behaviors. She was able to note the frequency with which Tyler exhibited skill in finding "chunks" or phonograms within words to help himself, monitored and self-corrected his miscues, and cross-checked one cue against the other. The records revealed his growing independence as a reader, and his teacher was able to scaffold Tyler's learning to the next levels through specific demonstrations and careful selection of text that would present new challenges for his learning.

Any assessment tool has its limitations in terms of the type of information it can provide. We might assume from children's ability to read expressively that they understand what is being read, but when very early readers are busy processing text, they do not always employ a great deal of expression during oral reading. As powerful as running records can be in telling about the strategies young children use to decode text,

Figure 1
Tyler's Running Record

Page	Running Record of Child's Reading	Printed Text
2	√√√√ √√	Did you fee my cow? Yes, Ma'am.
3	<u>What/SC</u> √√√√ Will √√	Will you tell me how? Yes, Ma'am.
4	√√√√ √√√	What did you feed her? Corn and hay.
5	√√√√ √√√	What did you feed her? Corn and hay.
6	√√√ <u>the/SC</u> <u>cow</u> her too √√	Did you milk her, too? Yes, Ma'am.
7	√√√√ √√√ √√√√ √√√	How did you milk her? Swish, swish, swish. How did you milk her? Swish, swish, swish
8	√√√ √√ √√ √√√ √√	Did you feed my pony? Yes, Ma'am. Did my pony eat? Yes, Ma'am.
9	√√√ <u>sloppy</u> <u>sloppy</u> sloppity, sloppity √√√ <u>sloppy</u> <u>sloppy</u> sloppity slop	How did he eat? Sloppity, sloppity. How did he eat? Sloppity, slop!

they cannot provide insights into a child's overall understanding of a story. To tap into a child's comprehension of what he or she reads, teachers can look at the information provided during a story retelling (see Chapter 3 for further discussion of comprehension strategies).

Story Retellings

We know quite a bit about Tyler's growing skill in word identification, but literacy is so much more than that. A balanced approach to literacy education requires that we look at Tyler's knowledge and ability in a number of other areas, including his ability to construct meaning from text. We can learn about his comprehension of story through retellings.

Story retellings (Morrow, 1993) are a wonderful assessment for two main reasons. First, they can tell a great deal about children's comprehension; second, they are as much an instructional tool as they are an assessment. The child benefits in a number of ways every time he or she engages in a retelling, which certainly cannot be said of all assessments. Story retellings can alleviate the concerns of the teacher who worries that some forms of assessment take time away from the learning process. When a child is asked to do a retelling, he or she becomes engaged in tasks requiring use of oral language, recall, and comprehension of narrative text.

To conduct a retelling with a child, teachers must first make decisions about what they want to discover. It is not simply a matter of deciding to do the assessment and then conducting it to see what happens. The usefulness of this assessment depends on one's purpose in conducting the retellings; without establishing that purpose beforehand a teacher may be uncertain about what the results of the retelling represent.

There are a number of factors that must be considered when planning to conduct story retellings: they can be done at practically any age or grade level; they can be done with or without the text in front of the child; they can be done orally or in written form; they can be done with a text that was read to the child or a text that the child read alone; and they can be done with the same text across different retelling settings or with a different text each time. Deciding which of these circumstances is appropriate depends on what the teacher seeks to gain from the retelling event. If a child is not yet attending to print, but the teacher wants to know if the child can weave a story across the pages in a book in which the illustrations carry the storyline (Sulzby, 1985), certainly it is appropriate for the child to refer to the illustrations during the retelling process. The ability of emergent readers to gain meaning from picture cues is an important indicator of their level of reading development. With children who are able to read the text, you may decide that it is more appropriate to have them retell without the aid of the pictures. It is important to note, however, that such retellings depend on the child's ability to recall the story; memory of the story just read or heard is really a part of what is being assessed.

With the young child who is an emergent reader, teachers and adult caregivers often overhear a spontaneous retelling of a favorite story. The child turns the pages and uses the illustrations and memory for the story to retell it in much the same way as it was read by an adult. Children enjoy revisiting good stories in this fashion, and the process of retelling the story draws from the child's sense of book language, book handling, function and purpose of print, and understanding of the storyline. Every new opportunity to engage in such retellings extends the child's emerging understandings.

As Tyler grew into a beginning reader and was able to access text independently, use of retellings kept both Tyler and his teacher focused on meaning making as the ultimate result of an encounter with text. As first graders struggle to decode, the sense of story may be lost as children's energies and attention are devoted to deciphering print. But reading as a meaning-making proposition must be reinforced at all stages of a reader's development, and this is where retellings can be particularly useful. If the child has the understanding that a retelling will be expected after his reading, he will approach the reading event in a different fashion than a child who has no such expectation. This is true for any reader, as even an older child will quickly decide for himself what the teacher expects and will read according to the purpose as he perceives it. This perceived purpose may not be the purpose the teacher has in mind. For this reason, the child needs to know in advance that he will be asked to "tell about the story" afterward. This advance warning signals the child that he must pay attention to the storyline.

With children in upper-primary to intermediate grades, sometimes the way in which retellings are conducted is as much a factor of the classroom's daily schedule as the kind of information the teacher is attempting to assess. How does a teacher listen to 25 individual children retell the stories they have read? Time is a critical consideration in any elementary classroom. Those teachers who employ a reader's workshop approach to their classrooms can structure the opportunity to listen to retellings during individual conferences with children. Other teachers who use grouping arrangements to teach with basals or trade books will probably have fewer opportunities to meet individually with children and may find that using written retellings is useful. The caution in the latter situation is that children who struggle as writers may not be able to express their understanding of stories in writing as effectively as they can orally. For this reason, it would be ideal if a blend of both oral and written retellings could be used across the school year.

Oral retellings can take too much valuable instructional time if children ramble through retellings that include every detail in the story. This is the way primary children approach retellings because this is the only way they know, and their idea of "telling the story" is that one should remember and relay everything that comes to mind. Because a good retelling should contain all the most important components of the story, use of a story map can help children be focused and concise in retellings. One strategy a teacher might employ is to have a story-map format at the table when a child comes for a conference. The child refers to each part of the map in retelling the story and soon learns to highlight only the most important features of a story. Or, the child might be asked to illustrate the major story parts and to write about each.

A simple story map with just four components—place, characters, problem, and ending—is suitable to prompt the retellings of emergent and beginning readers. A pictorial representation for the map works very well, as demonstrated by Tyler's work shown in Figure 2.

Figure 2
Tyler's Story Map for *There's Something in My Attic*

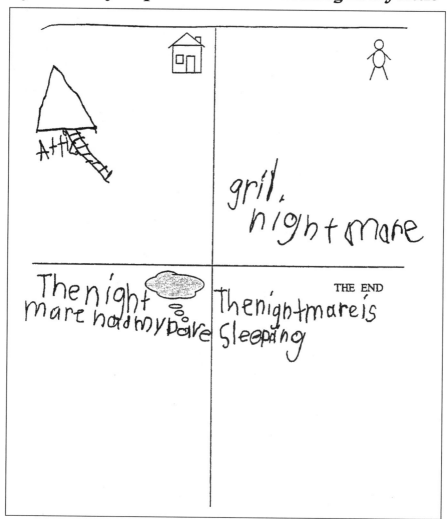

Tyler had made significant gains in reading by the time he drew this map in the spring of the year and had nearly caught up with his first-grade class in reading. He displayed his understanding of the main parts of *There's Something in My Attic* (Mayer, 1988) after he read the book for the second time. The little house icon reminds Tyler to tell and/or draw where the story took place. (Asking for setting from emergent and beginning readers probably should not include when the story happened, because time is an abstract concept for young children.) Tyler drew a set of stairs and a pitched roof, and wrote the word *Attic*. The stick figure icon reminds him to tell about and/or draw the main characters in the story; Tyler simply writes *gril* (girl) and *nightmare*, the latter word copied directly from the text. The dark cloud icon represents the problem. Tyler writes, *The night mare had my bare*, adopting the perspective of the girl in the story whose teddy bear had been taken by the nightmare. Finally, the words *The End* instruct Tyler to tell or draw how the story ended. Tyler simply writes, *The nightmare is sleeping.*

Tyler had decided that drawing was going to take too much time, so he decided to write his responses for each of the parts of the story map. This shows how far Tyler has come since the start of the year when he could only use drawing to represent ideas and adamantly refused to write because he was sure he did not know how. Now Tyler chooses to write as a quick and efficient way to express himself. He does not elaborate in his writing, but he is gaining control over writing as a communication tool and is not afraid to use it.

By looking at his map, we can observe what Tyler knows about this story. He can correctly identify the setting, the main characters, and the problem. He is not quite as successful in describing the resolution; he relates an event at the end of the book, but does not quite resolve the story. However, it is quite evident that Tyler understands the "gist" of the narrative. We also can learn something about his writing and spelling development from the map, particularly as we continue to gather samples of his work over a period of time.

As children progress through the grades and more complex understanding of narrative is expected, the story map gains additional components: the aspect of time is added to setting, the main character's goal becomes an important feature, characters' personality traits may be asked for, and main events or theme might be added. The elements asked for in the retelling should parallel those elements of the story that are considered appropriate for children to learn at a given grade level.

Retellings, of course, are done after a child has completed the reading of a text. Like most postreading assessments, there is an element of recall that needs to be taken into account. And tapping into recall does not always capture what was going through the child's mind during the actual reading event. Another variation on the retelling is to have the child conduct a "think-aloud" during the actual process of reading. Because think-alouds require some skill and sophistication on the part of the student, they are more appropriate for older children like Andrew.

Assessing Andrew's Literacy Skills

Think-Alouds During Reading

With Andrew, a capable reader who primarily engages in silent reading, word identification and comprehension of literacy-level details are rarely an issue. Some of the more important questions are whether or not he is able to relate his background knowledge to what he is reading, to read for varied purposes, to use reading to gain information, to engage in mental imagery, and to enter into a transaction with the text on a personal level (Rosenblatt, 1978). Although reading processes may be readily evident in the oral reading of beginners, they go underground in the silent reading of older, capable readers, and we are left to guess which strategies the child chooses to employ.

Think-alouds are windows into children's minds. They reveal a tremendous amount of information about all the ways in which a child engages in sense-making during a reading event. Rather than tapping into (or testing) recall, as retellings tend to do, the think-aloud provides information about a child's thought processes during the reading of text because there is less emphasis on memory and more on cognitive processing.

Perhaps the most important piece of advice for a teacher in regard to conducting a think-aloud is to remain as silent as possible, to allow the child to express what is going through her mind. Too many questions or prompts may lead the child to tell you what you want to hear. The think-aloud is best done if the child is part way into the book, and has already built a sense of the story. Beginning at a particular point in the story, have the child tell you what is going through her mind as she reads. Again, such an oral sharing of the story will require time set aside in a one-on-one conference, but you will discover a great deal about a young reader in the process.

It is interesting that even though Andrew is a fourth grader, he is still very interested in picture books despite the fact that he is quite capable of reading the much more advanced text in lengthy chapter books. It is possible, however, to gain quite a bit of information about what this child knows and can do by listening to his spontaneous sharing of an easy (for him) picture book. Take, for example, Andrew's reading of *The Tree That Would Not Die* (Levine, 1995). Levine chronicles the story of the magnificent, 400-year-old Treaty Oak in Austin, Texas, as scenes from historical events are played out beneath its branches. The following transcript shows Andrew's delight in the story and illustrations and his careful thinking and understanding of what he has read. Andrew was simply asked to tell about what he was reading. The transcript of his think-aloud contains things he says about the book during the actual reading event, interspersed with periods of silent reading. Occasionally there is a teacher question or prompt. Andrew begins discussing the story about a third of the way into the book:

Andrew: It's about a tree, and it's telling the story. It's hundreds of years ago, and an acorn fell, and that's who the tree is, and it grows. It tells about Indians and Spanish settlers, and a buffalo, and a bluejay. I imagine the tree will be hundreds of years old at the end. It was spared from the settlers for building houses because it was a landmark between the settlers and the Indians.

(Silent reading of the text continues.)

Hey! This story takes place in the Southwest. This could be extra credit!

Reads aloud:	"I was very large when I got word that Sam Houston and his soldiers had defeated the Mexican Army." (Silent reading continues.) Look how they spelled Texas (*Tejas*). Probably because it's in Mexico right now (referring to the era in the story).
	(Reads silently) Austin! Remember for a certain story I held up a picture of Texas? (a reference to a presentation on U.S. states, given in third grade.)
(Reads silently.)	
	"People owning people—how can that be?" I like how the tree puts that.
Teacher:	Why?
Andrew:	It's not right to own slaves. (Reads on in the text.) Oh! The tree saves two boys from being captured. There are two boys, one Mexican, one black. The tree tells the owl to be quiet so the people don't find them, and they escape.
(Reads on silently.)	
	Oh—we're studying this in social studies—the cattle ranching. The tree is afraid now, because people are talking about cutting it down.
(Reads silently.)	
	Oh, the tree thinks that the children saved him because the children sent pennies and nickels. The city built a park around the tree.
(Reads silently.)	
(Pointing to the next illustration)	
	Look how big the tree got! Here's the same picture as on the cover. A lot of books have that.
(Turning to next page)	
	Uh-oh. Look what's happening.

Teacher:	What?
Andrew:	I don't know. They might be hurting the tree. I don't know. (Reads on.)

(Several pages later)

It's probably a monument now, because the tree is so old and big. (Reading farther in the text.) The tree is dying now, I think. But because of a person, I don't think it will die.

(Reading on. Finally, he points to the young tree in the illustration on the last page, and smiles broadly.)

Although Andrew has touched on major events in the story, it's not clear if he understood what happened to the tree.

Teacher:	Do you know why the tree got sick?
Andrew:	Yeah. The tree was poisoned by a guy who wanted to kill it. People gave money to help it and scientists came and the tree was saved, even though they had to cut branches off it.... I'd like to see that tree sometime.
Teacher:	Why?
Andrew:	I'd just like to see what it looks like now. It would be cool to see it.
Teacher:	Do you think this is a good book?
Andrew:	Yeah. Stories about trees aren't usually interesting, but this one is interesting.
Teacher:	Why?
Andrew:	The author really made it interesting by having the tree tell the story.

It is immediately apparent that Andrew did far more than simply recall details; he engages in divergent thinking and personal response to literature. He makes connections with previous and current learning ("Oh—we're studying this in social studies—the cattle ranching.");

predicts what will happen in the story ("I imagine the tree will be hundreds of years old at the end."); engages in inferential thinking ("Look how they spelled Texas (*Tejas*). Probably because it's in Mexico...."); demonstrates his knowledge of picture books ("A lot of books have that.") and his appreciation of the author's craft ("The author really made it interesting by having the tree tell the story."); relates the story to his personal experience ("I'd like to see that tree sometime."); and displays an aesthetic stance toward the reading event ("'People owning people—how can that be?' I like how the tree puts that.") All this was captured with scarcely a word from the teacher; Andrew only needed a few simple prompts ("What?" "Why?") to elaborate on things he had said. In addition, anecdotal notes taken during the think-aloud capture his body language during the process: Andrew is excited and eagerly turns each page to see what will happen next. He shares the story in an animated fashion. Clearly, he is very engaged in the reading of the book.

The rich information about Andrew as a reader that can be captured in a think-aloud is helpful for making decisions about supporting his literacy learning. In addition, just the fact that someone sat down to hear him describe his thinking during a story he so obviously enjoys is a motivating factor for a child who does not usually read for purposes of enjoyment. This underscores the power of retellings and think-alouds as assessment tools that are of direct benefit to the learner; the act of retelling or of thinking-aloud serves to activate comprehension and meaning making. But it is also important to note that children who are not familiar with think-alouds will first require teacher modeling and demonstration so that they understand their task in the think-aloud.

Gathering and Documenting Information

Retellings or think-alouds can be documented in several ways. An audiotape, checklist, teacher's notes on a story map, or a written retelling are all possibilities. The checklist and the story map are assessment tools because they directly relate to the specific features of the story that the teacher is looking for.

The teacher might choose to use audiotapes, one per child in the classroom. The tapes could include both oral reading samples as well as retelling samples, and could be done periodically throughout the school year. An accompanying record card notes the child's name, date of each sample, and the title (and level, if desired) of the story read or retold. Such tapes are wonderful tools to use at parent-teacher conferences to help parents become aware of their children's progress. The tapes also could become part of a literacy portfolio.

A checklist could be devised to use during the retelling event at an individual conference with the child. The more that can be done during the retelling itself, to avoid after-the-fact record keeping, the better it will be. Too much is lost by trying to reconstruct information later, and other things can get in the way of returning to record keeping at the end of the school day.

Assessing Attitudes, Habits, and Interests

The only child of parents who talk with him and expose him to lots of places and experiences, Andrew has tremendous world knowledge on many topics and loves to share his information with the rest of the class. He brings his new microscope to share on the day when he is class leader. He will readily talk about an amazing piece of information he and his dad picked up from the Discovery Channel, or he will pull out a book from the Eyewitness series of nature books to show all about the differences between alligators and crocodiles. His bookshelves at home are filled with good children's literature, both fiction and nonfiction. Sometimes Andrew checks out books from the school library; usually these are books about insects, reptiles, or mammals. He samples pieces of these books, looking at the pictures and reading parts that intrigue him. But if his mother did not enforce reading time at night, Andrew probably would not read a book of his own accord. He will read for the 30 minutes she insists on, then immediately stop reading, even if he is in the middle of a sentence. He likes to hear stories read to him, but rarely checks out fiction books to read for pleasure. As was explained earlier, he is more likely to pick up an easier picture book with compelling illustrations than to choose a chapter book for its compelling storyline.

Most teachers would say they want more for their students than simply to be able to read. They want children to choose to read because they enjoy reading. Teachers who believe in a balanced approach not only want to help children become readers, they also want to foster the love of reading and encourage children to become lifelong readers. Is it enough to say a child can read, if he will not read? Classroom teachers invest a great deal of time and energy in stimulating children's love of reading, through sharing a wealth of good literature, modeling positive reading behaviors, providing silent reading time, doing daily read alouds, and initiating book talks. But what effect does all this sustained, concerted effort have on the students? We need to be able to see the results and document shifts in children's habits and attitudes toward reading in some fashion. Surveys and inventories can be extremely useful in this regard, particularly if administered at the beginning and again at the end of the school year.

Many teachers have used published reading attitude/habit/interest inventories and have found them to be useful. It is difficult to come up with a universal instrument that addresses what the individual child thinks about reading; however, many instruments designed to tap into children's reading attitudes, habits, and interests can reveal interesting information that one might not otherwise discover about a child. However, it is not the assessment tool itself that is so important; it is the fact that the teacher sits down to talk with the child one-on-one. In addition to the answers to the questions themselves, a teacher might be well-advised to take anecdotal notes on the things the child has to say for reasons behind his or her answers. (As with any anecdotal notes, it is important to note only those things that are directly observed or said, without adding any layer of judgment or interpretation.) The following dialogue shows Andrew's thoughts on books and reading.

Teacher: What do you do when you come to a word you don't know?

Andrew: I try to sound it out to see if it's a word I know but I don't know how to spell. I try to sound it out with the parts, and if it doesn't make sense, I usually ask.

Teacher: What if no one's around to ask?

Andrew: I read around it and try to figure out what it is.

Teacher: If you knew a little kid who wondered what reading was, what would you tell him?

Andrew: It's sounding out words to make stories and sentences and paragraphs to tell things.

Teacher: What's reading for?

Andrew: You can read books just for fun to see what happens in them. It can be for fun and it can be something you have to do.

Teacher: Tell me a book you really like.

Andrew: I really liked *Matilda*. It was just a real interesting book. It had special things. I just can't explain.

Teacher: Who's your favorite author?

Andrew: I don't really know that many people that write books.

Teacher: How is reading a storybook different from reading social studies or science?

Andrew: You usually read storybooks a lot faster because social studies and science have words you don't really know and you want to find a lot of information. And you learn things in social studies and science.

Teacher: What do you like to read about?

Andrew: Interesting books. I usually don't like most true books as much as fiction. Fiction you don't know what's going to happen next. Anything can happen in a fiction book. I also do like some autobiographies.

Teacher: What kinds of books do you usually check out?

Andrew: At school I check out fact books about animals. At the library for town I usually check out fiction books.

Teacher: Do you like to read?

Andrew: Yes. There are so many different things in books. You can see what you want to—you don't have to watch TV to see them; you can imagine them how you want.

Teacher: How do you know if a book is going to be a good one?

Andrew: I usually read the back cover.

Teacher: How could I get you to read more?

Andrew: If I could find a whole bunch of really good books that I was really interested in, I would read more.

Note Andrew's skills-based orientation to the act of reading ("It's sounding out words..."). This might be a cause for concern if he were not such a capable reader who attends to meaning. Other comments by Andrew suggest that he is beyond mere "sounding out" and can experience reading from an aesthetic stance ("You can see what you want to...you can imagine..."). Andrew also understands the differences between narrative and expository text and knows how to adjust his rate to the reading of different types of text ("You usually read storybooks a lot faster...").

It is probably not surprising that Andrew does not recognize many authors of children's books; there is no consistent read-aloud program in place in his school above the primary level. Even though he is expected to read at home, he does not engage in conversations about authors with his family. It is surprising, however, that he enjoys fiction more than nonfiction, given the choices he makes when checking out books from the school library. It may be that selecting a visually appealing nonfiction book about insects or animals gave Andrew a quick means to fulfill a teacher expectation that he select a book during library time. Andrew has read a number of books by Roald Dahl and truly enjoyed them; to help him select other books by an author that he enjoys would be a place to start. Building on his exposure to Dahl's writing might help Andrew find that "bunch of really good books" that would whet his appetite for more.

Reading Logs

One other tool that might help Andrew become more aware of authors and to start to feel successful as a reader is for him to keep a reading log of the books he has completed. Logs such as these are useful with younger children like Tyler as well, but because young children read so many little books in such a relatively short amount of time, it would be a daunting task to list every book read. In that case, children might select a single day's or week's best book, and date the entry. Over time, both child and teacher have a sense of developing taste in literature and growing expertise with more and more challenging material. Such a log conveys a wonderful sense of accomplishment, and children can share it proudly with their parents at conference time. These types of records can be kept on their own or may become part of a literacy portfolio.

The Literacy Portfolio

As a classroom teacher, I always kept a file folder of children's work to share with parents at conference time, and so did almost every other teacher I worked with. But these were not portfolios. A portfolio is far more than just a collection of a child's work (Leslie & Jett-Simpson, 1997; Tierney, Carter, & Desai, 1991).

Perhaps the portfolio concept can be summarized in an experience I had with a fifth-grade class I taught long ago, before portfolios were used as an assessment tool. At that time I was a bit of a fanatic on handwriting. Every quarter, I had my students copy the same paragraph from the chalkboard in their best handwriting, and date it. I kept the papers until the end of the year and in the last week of school I passed them out to the students. They would lay the papers on their desks in chronological order and look over what they had done over the year. Invariably, a number of students would exclaim, "Wow! Look at how much better my writing is now than it used to be!" Now handwriting looms less large on my teaching agenda, but the memory of my students' reactions has stayed with me. They assessed their own work and self-evaluated their progress, rather than waiting for me to stamp them with a grade. That is what a good portfolio can do, and it should include goal-setting on the part of the student. We hope the student will be able to tell himself or herself, "If this is what I see in my work, then this is where I want to go in my own learning."

Active learning, engagement, motivation, self-evaluation, and goal-setting all are part and parcel of the portfolio concept. But where does a teacher start? There are so many issues to consider: What goes into portfolios? Where should they be stored? Who decides which pieces to include? Do they get passed on to next year's teacher?

Before embarking on a portfolio project, the teacher would be well-advised to keep three things in mind: (1) be sure to introduce portfolios carefully to your students, (2) start small, and (3) be sure to provide time for individual periodical conferences with your students. If these three considerations are not addressed, portfolio efforts are likely to fail.

Contents of a Portfolio

What goes into a literacy portfolio? Again, you need to consider your purpose. Is this a portfolio that will be passed on to next year's teachers to apprise them of the level of achievement in reading and writing reached by the children who will enter their classes in the fall? Or is this a portfolio designed to invite students into the evaluation process and to help them develop an awareness of their own learning and growth? In the first instance, you might decide that some teacher-created documents ought to be passed along, such as checklists, anecdotal records, and audiotapes; in the second instance, these things probably would not appear within the portfolio. In either case, however, a variety of documents and ways of capturing students' learning ought to be considered. Written work samples, creative writing, oral reading tapes, a list of books read or favorite books, and student responses to reading, writing, and strategy interviews are just a few of the documents that could be included.

There are countless times when students complete large-scale group projects that say a great deal about their learning, and we know that once the display comes down the record of the learning will be gone. And yet we realize that children's developing skills in cooperative work and social interaction are powerful elements of their learning and growth that we might also need and want to capture. Pictures taken of such projects could be included in children's portfolios, so teachers should keep a camera handy.

Management of Portfolios

Teachers who involve students in the management of portfolios will do themselves a tremendous favor, and benefit children in the process. Children—even young children—can handle the regular management of a portfolio very well once they know how it works. To capture the child's development over time, teachers should date every piece that is included. Involve the children in dating, filing, and organizing the portfolio. Even kindergartners can manage to use a date stamp on their papers—and they usually enjoy it.

Children can be active managers of the portfolios as long as the portfolio pieces are located in an accessible place in the classroom—perhaps on a rolling file cart with hanging folders or in a file drawer or box—so that children's work can be added or removed at will. A "working portfolio" contains works-in-progress and finished pieces as they are completed. The working portfolio can be culled at conference time to narrow it to a "best piece" portfolio, especially if that is what you intend to send on to the next teacher.

Selection of Contents

Choosing which pieces of evidence give a well-rounded picture of a child's development and achievement is not always a simple thing to do. The issue of what goes into a child's portfolio can be considered in the following scenario:

It is the end of the school day. The children have just received their papers from you, papers that you have carefully read, evaluated, and graded. Julie, in particular, has done an outstanding job. Her piece is brief, as usual, but she uses very descriptive language. You tell the class to be sure to take their papers home to show their parents. The buses have pulled out, and the neighborhood children leave the room to begin the walk home. You see Julie crumple what you consider to be her exemplary work and toss it in the wastepaper basket as she goes by. You wonder: Why wouldn't Julie want to take that paper home? You know her parents would be thrilled to see it, so that is not the problem.

Who was invested in Julie's paper? The teacher, more than any other person. Who decided its worth? The teacher. If Julie had had a say in determining which pieces go into a portfolio, she might well have chosen that piece, but then again, maybe not. Children may have very different, but nonetheless legitimate, reasons for choosing the pieces that exemplify their best work. Julie's favorite piece might be selected by her because it was about unicorns and she is fascinated with unicorns. You, on the other hand, might not select that piece because it is not as successful or as representative of her developing skill as a writer as is the piece with the colorful description that she wrote about her pet cat. This will call for some negotiation skills and compromise. In a shared view of the child's learning, both teacher and child voices must be heard. The teacher cannot wholly abdicate his or her expert view of the child's learning, but the child's own appraisal of his or her work cannot be ignored; it must be fostered and encouraged.

With very young children, selection can be a problem for a very different reason. To young children, everything they do is wonderful. Kindergarten and first-grade children often find it very difficult to choose the very best from among several pieces of their work. Rather than force them to make decisions they are not ready to make, it is far better to send home the pieces on a regular basis and just make copies of those samples that you believe to be the most revealing about the child's growth and development.

Ownership

My belief is that for the individual teacher and his or her classroom the benefits of portfolios are so strong that even if others do not buy into the concept, a teacher could "go it alone" and still reap the benefits of using portfolios. In fact, in many instances it is best if portfolios do not become too institutionalized. Many large-scale portfolio attempts have taken the immediacy and the personal element out of portfolios, and they become overly prescribed by external decision makers. It is far better to keep the portfolio within one's own classroom, and to help students achieve a level of self-evaluation and goal setting without having to worry about outside evaluation, which may begin to drive the process and product in ways that neither you nor your students would desire. Once it is dictated what must go into a portfolio, the portfolio belongs to someone else. Whose portfolio is it, anyway? It should belong to the student, first, last, and always.

Goal Setting

Perhaps the greatest benefit that can be realized by incorporating portfolios into a classroom is that of self-evaluation and goal setting on the part of the student. Of course, this is related to conferencing and selection issues. As children consider which pieces represent their best work, evaluation of their work and progress is going on. The children might be asked to write a simple paragraph or a few lines about why they chose each piece and what it says about their learning.

Careful groundwork must be laid to help children understand what is involved in setting a goal, and to help them set reasonable, manageable goals. Conversation in class could begin with the times in children's lives when they set goals for themselves, such as in learning to ride a bike, passing a level in swimming class, or advancing to the next level in karate. Examples of short-term, achievable goals in the classroom should be given, such as remembering to put your name on your paper today, or putting materials away neatly after a work period. After the children have a chance to set simple goals and can announce that they achieved them, it is much easier to move on to academic goals. Examples of things that can be accomplished in short order are helpful before moving to broader, more long-term goals such as writing and publishing a story for the Young Author's Fair. As children experience success with simple goals, the motivation to set and work toward meaningful literacy goals is heightened.

Informal Assessment in the Elementary Classroom: A Teacher's Questions

Many of the excellent ideas found in the literature on informal assessments are the kinds of things professional educators want and need to try in the context of their classrooms. However, even though the literature reports successes people have had with informal assessments, there still are a number of critical questions that classroom teachers ask frequently.

Where do I start?

Start at the beginning with one small step. Most importantly, start with something you are really interested in trying. The danger can lie in attempting too much, too soon. Try just one new thing, give it plenty of time, and then step back to take a careful look at how well it has worked for you.

What if I don't get the results that are described in the literature?

You are just beginning. What is described in the literature represents a model; in some instances, it is an ideal to strive toward. The writer often presents the best-case scenario and you are left to wonder why your attempts look nothing like it. What you read may not always give you a clear picture of the struggles that teachers go through on their way to creating the final product or achieving the results you are reading about. However, it is good to have the ideal in mind so that you know how much you can achieve.

My students are not reacting to this assessment in the ways I had hoped they would. Now what do I do?

Talk to your students. Tell them what you are trying to accomplish, and why. Hear what they have to say. This all assumes that you spent a good deal of time at the outset preparing children for what they could expect with this new approach. But even if you forgot that all-important step, you can still salvage the process later by stopping to talk with your class. Ask the children

- Is this helping you?
- What might work better?
- What do you think about how you are learning?
- What do you know how to do?
- What do you need to work on?

We cannot examine a child's learning apart from the child's view of himself as a learner. In other words, if you do not go straight to the source you will neglect aspects of a child's learning that he could supply easily—if one would only ask.

Sometimes children are not necessarily able to recognize what is useful for them. Take Tyler, for example. When he was stuck on a difficult word that could not be figured out by any other means, he was encouraged to skip it and read to the end of the sentence to see if he could then return to the word and decode it. He resisted this approach at first and could be heard saying emphatically, "That doesn't help me!" Tyler simply was not ready to make use of the strategy at that point. The interesting thing, however, is that Tyler was even able to take that view of the situation; he was able to think about what worked or did not work for him. It was, in some respects, quite encouraging to see this evidence of metacognition coming from a child who struggled as a learner.

I've been trying so hard to put this assessment into place, but it's taking up so much of my time that I'm beginning to wonder if it's all worth it.

If you are exhausting yourself in the process, clearly some adjustments need to be made. Are you attempting too much at once? Where could you cut back? It is far better to concentrate on becoming comfortable with one piece of the total picture before attempting more. We cannot allow an assessment practice or tool to become so cumbersome that we drop it—it needs to be intertwined with classroom practice and not thought of as an add-on.

If you are trying to get samples of children's oral reading, think-alouds, or retellings during the school day, you know that it is difficult to find the time to squeeze them in. Unless you have planned ahead for quiet reading or writing time for the other children in the room, there will be inevitable interruptions of any one-on-one conference time. Your entire class needs to understand the significance of conference time and how important it is for them to be independent workers until you are finished with a conference. Plan to meet with children on a rotating basis so that you can conference with every child in the room within a period of several weeks.

Time, of course, is an important consideration in any classroom. However, the biggest concern is not whether the assessment itself is time-consuming; the real issue is whether classroom instruction is wasting the teacher's and children's time, because good assessment might have shown that some of the instruction was not necessary in the first place.

I'm really excited about all these great ideas and I'm going to revamp my whole assessment program.

Take stock. What kinds of things are you already doing that give you good information about children? Do these assessments provide information that helps you design instruction to move children forward as readers and writers? If so, why would you ever want to stop doing something so useful? The reality is, you simply cannot do it all. So find your middle ground or comfort zone. This is not to suggest a complacent kind of comfortable, but rather a place where you feel secure in the types of things you already are doing so that you are free to experiment with new things.

Tyler and Andrew: A Final Word

The school year is nearly over and both boys have learned a great deal. Their teachers, taking a balanced approach to literacy assessment, have learned a great deal about the boys, as well. So what progress have the boys made? Tyler, thankfully, has been successfully discontinued from the early intervention program and is exiting first grade a competent reader. He has a number of strategies to help himself and is quite independent in his use of those strategies. He should manage second-grade reading and writing quite nicely. Andrew has matured, and with the combined efforts of a caring teacher who closely monitored his work and parents who established strict ground rules about homework, he has been successful in completing his work on time and in a much more organized fashion. There is also reason to believe that he will be able to spend more time reading at home now that his evenings are not taken up with completing late work. Both boys are very proud of their successes.

Perhaps the best assessment of all is Tyler's final comment as he walked out of the classroom one day. His teacher said to him, "Tyler, I'm proud of you! You are getting to be such a good reader."

His reply? "I *am* a good reader!"

And that's what it's all about.

REFERENCES

Clay, M.M. (1993). *An observational survey of early literacy development.* Portsmouth, NH: Heinemann.

Clay, M.M. (1994). *Reading Recovery: A guidebook for teachers in training.* Portsmouth, NH: Heinemann.

Ferreiro, E. (1986). The interplay between information and assimilation in beginning literacy. In W.H. Teale & E. Sulzby (Eds.), *Emergent literacy: Writing and reading* (pp. 15–49). Norwood, NJ: Ablex.

Jett-Simpson, M., & Greenewald, M.J. (1996). *Short and long-term impact of ERE staff development training on teachers' beliefs, practices and dispositions.* Paper presented at annual meeting of the National Reading Conference, Charleston, SC.

Johnston, P.H. (1997). *Knowing literacy: Constructive literacy assessment.* York, ME: Stenhouse.

Leslie, L., & Jett-Simpson, M. (Eds.). (1997). *Authentic literacy assessment: An ecological approach.* New York: Addison-Wesley Longman.

Morrow, L.M. (1993). *Literacy development in the early years* (2nd ed.). Englewood Cliffs, NJ: Prentice Hall.

Rosenblatt, L. (1978). *The reader, the text, the poem.* Carbondale, IL: Southern Illinois University Press.

Sulzby, E. (1985). Children's emergent reading of favorite storybooks: A developmental study. *Reading Research Quarterly, 20,* 458–481.

Tierney, R.J., Carter, M.A., & Desai, L.E. (1991). *Portfolio assessment in the reading-writing classroom.* Norwood, MA: Christopher-Gordon.

CHILDREN'S LITERATURE REFERENCES

Dahl, R. (1988). *Matilda.* London: Jonathon Cape.

Levine, E. (1995). *The tree that would not die.* New York: Scholastic.

Mayer, M. (1988). *There's something in my attic.* New York: Penguin.

Melser, J. (1985). *Yes, Ma'am.* Bothell, WA: The Wright Group.

CHAPTER 6

■ ■ ■

Achieving a Balance in First-Grade Instruction

E. Jo Ann Belk

When should reading begin? What is the best method of teaching reading? How is this determined? Becoming a fluent reader is the key to being successful in school and later in life (Burns, Roe, & Ross, 1999). Children who have early success in school are more likely to develop positive self-concepts and to continue in school rather than drop out (Carbo, 1996a). Reading skills developed by children will give them a foundation for future learning. As teachers we want our students to have the best instruction available to enable them to become fluent readers. The purpose of this chapter is to help teachers to provide the best reading instruction possible based on research and best practices. Research on reading methods is presented in the first part of the chapter. This research supports a balanced approach to teaching reading that includes components from the literature approach, phonics, and writing. Another important aspect of teaching reading is the actual classroom application of a particular reading method. Some methods sound promising in theory but in order to determine the effectiveness of a method it should be implemented in an actual classroom setting. The second part of the chapter includes a classroom application of a balanced approach to teaching reading. Written by Beth Reeves, a first-grade teacher, the narrative demonstrates an effective way to include all the components of a balanced approach to teaching reading, including phonemic awareness, phonics, literature, oral language development, and writing.

The Importance of Reading

Most authorities agree that the initial period of formal reading instruction, usually kindergarten and first grade, is the most critical. When children succeed in reading at the beginning of their schooling, they develop positive attitudes toward reading and learning that greatly influence their chance of future success in school in all subject areas. If they experience failure during this critical period, it can be very difficult for them to catch up (Carbo, 1996a; Stanovich, 1986). Pikulski (1997) determined that first-grade reading achievement is a good predictor of later reading achievement and that children who are not competent readers by third grade are likely to have reading difficulties for life.

Teaching children to read provides a challenging task for the kindergarten and first-grade teachers. All good teachers want to provide the best possible instruction to ensure their students become able and competent readers. To accomplish this objective, the National Research Council found that components from both phonics and whole languages approaches were critical in helping children to become competent readers (Smith, Stevenson, & Li, 1998).

The importance of helping children become competent readers was recognized by the 1998 U.S. National Reading Summit. U.S. Secretary of Education Richard Riley noted that 44% of fourth graders read below grade level. He emphasized the goal of helping all children develop strong literacy skills. The summit recommended that parents help children become competent readers by reading daily to them from infancy, and that teachers use a variety of teaching methods and provide more help for children with limited English, with disabilities, and from lower socioeconomic homes (U.S. Department of Education, 1998). As the contributors to this volume emphasize, teachers must be knowledgeable of the children they teach, methods of teaching, and current research on best practices of reading instruction.

Honig (1997) reviewed research concerning best practices in reading instruction. He found that successful reading teachers used proven components from whole language and organized skill development components such as phonemic awareness, phonics, and decoding.

Honig listed 10 components of a comprehensive reading strategy: (1) an intensive oral language program, (2) a writing program stressing narrative and expository writing, (3) phonological decoding skills, (4) ongoing diagnostic assessment and intervention, (5) independent reading, (6) advanced skill development, (7) reading strategies, (8) vocabulary development, (9) developmental spelling, and (10) parent and community involvement (pp. 8–9).

Emerging Literacy

At the turn of the 20th century, educators believed that a child was not ready for formal reading instruction until he or she reached a mental age of 6.5 years. The child then arrived at school ready to be introduced to reading by the first-grade teacher (Manzo & Manzo, 1995). We know now that emerging literacy begins at birth as children begin to focus on objects and recognize sounds (May, 1998). Most children acquire a rich and varied background of experiences that enable them to develop concepts necessary for reading. Other factors believed to influence successful reading acquisition include oral language development, phonemic awareness, concepts about print, and most importantly their home environment and parental influence (Heilman, Blair, & Rupley, 1998). Maggart and Zintz (1992) recognized several principles of literacy development: "Written language serves a variety of functions; oral language experiences impact on written language functions; context is a vital consideration in learning to read and write; and literacy is an emergent process" (p. 101).

Reading Instruction: A New Focus

The reading instruction pendulum has moved back and forth for most of the 20th century, and a new instructional focus has emerged in recent years. The emphasis is on a balanced approach that not only considers what needs to be learned, but looks at methods of instruction, how learning takes place, and the learners themselves (Morrow &

Tracey, 1997). Changing practices in the teaching of reading reflect new knowledge about learning and teaching. Strickland (1998) maintains that in a balanced literacy program, *how* you teach is as important as *what* you teach. Strickland lists five rules of thumb for maintaining a balanced literacy program:

1. Teach skills as a way to gain meaning. Skills are not ends in themselves.
2. Each day, include time for both guided instruction and independent work. Otherwise students will never internalize skills and make them their own.
3. Avoid teaching children as if they were empty receptacles for knowledge. Instead, allow them to build knowledge in a process-oriented way.
4. Integrate print and electronic materials effectively. That way, your classroom will reflect the multimedia world in which students live.
5. Always consider standardized test scores in light of informal assessment data. Encourage parents to do the same. (p. 4)

Carbo (1996b) also argues that teachers can improve reading programs by using a balanced approach. She gives the following suggestions for combining elements from different approaches:

1. Emphasize the fun of reading.
2. Recruit older children to make reading games for younger ones, including phonics games.
3. Do not allow youngsters to be referred to special education classes simply because they can't learn phonics.
4. Help teachers accumulate books and shelving for classroom libraries.
5. Encourage reading aloud to children daily.
6. Purchase tape players and blank cassettes so books can be recorded for youngsters.

7. Send teachers who are "movers and shakers" to some good reading seminars during the year.

8. Encourage both teachers and parents to learn and understand their children's reading styles. (p. 64)

In light of current research, educators have realized that an approach is needed that includes a combination of the best elements of instructional strategies from both whole language and phonics approaches, but encompasses much more than the addition of separate elements (Morgan, 1995; Weaver, 1998; see also Chapter 1 of this volume). Responding to the National Research Council's report *Preventing Reading Difficulties in Young Children* (Snow, Burns, & Griffin, 1998), Secretary Riley defined key elements children need in order to become fluent readers. He concluded that children need to learn letters and sounds, learn how to read for meaning, and have many opportunities to practice reading.

History of the Balanced Approach to Reading Instruction

As mentioned in the Introduction of this volume, in 1990 a group of educators from the United Kingdom formed an organization supporting a middle position concerning reading instruction. They formulated a philosophy supporting a balanced approach called "Balance, a Manifesto for Balance in the Teaching of Literacy and Language Skills" (Thompson, 1997). The members of the organization formulated principles to ensure balance in

- employing reading instructional approaches and open reading activity time,

- using code and meaning methodologies,

- employment of incidental one-on-one intervention strategies and development of planned lessons,

- using trade books and published teaching materials,
- using informal observations and formal assessing instruments, and
- use and awareness of language. (Thompson, 1997; see also the Introduction of this volume).

As a result of careful study of current research, several schools in the state of Georgia initiated a balanced approach to the teaching of reading. The approach included many elements of whole language such as classical stories, learning in context, and daily creative writing exercises. Additionally, direct instruction in phonics and other fundamental word recognition strategies were provided. Teachers immersed students in captivating children's literature and directly taught phonics each day according to a carefully sequenced plan (White, 1996). The reading program was structured to allow teachers to draw from their own specialties and the interests of the children. Emphasis was placed on deriving meaning from texts and motivating children to read. Reading scores improved in all schools using the program. One of these schools, Burruss Elementary School in Marietta, Georgia, was awarded the International Reading Association Exemplary Reading Program Award. These positive results support the work of Richgels, Poremba, and McGee (1996), who wrote, "A large body of research has strengthened the notion that phonemic awareness, beginning reading, and beginning writing go together" (p. 641). Many other researchers (see, for example, Carbo, 1996b; Diegmueller, 1996; Foorman, Frances, Navy, & Lebirman, 1991) stress the importance of using a combination of reading approaches to meet the different learning styles of children (1996). In a balanced approach children are systematically taught the relation between letters and sounds, and are encouraged to read interesting stories and write their own stories.

In the remainder of the chapter, Beth Reeves describes her first year of teaching first grade and how the balanced reading instruction approach she used helped her classroom of divergent learners become successful readers. Beth's approach to teaching reading is supported by research (for example, Heilman, Blair, & Rupley, 1998; Honig, 1997; Strickland, 1998). Through a "daily news" activity she addressed phonemic awareness, oral language development, writing, and reading. She used centers to incorporate basal, literature, and writing activities as well. The success of her teaching experience was both challenging and rewarding as illustrated by her children's reading skills at the end of the year.

A Balanced Reading Program Achieves Success: Beth's Story

After teaching second grade for 6 years, I felt like I needed a change. Second grade was a comfortable grade for me to teach; after all, the children came to me already knowing how to read and how to do some math. As a second-grade teacher, I basically built on the skills they already had. I decided to take a big step and become a first-grade teacher. After making the commitment to my principal, I began wondering if I had made a mistake. I asked myself, "How in the world am I going to teach these children how to read?" I had heard several comments from other first-grade teachers such as, "They won't know anything when they come to you and you will be lucky if half of them know all their letters." I also was told I would not have much time to spend on social studies and science. I was concerned that five basal readers were to be taught in the first grade; in second grade I only had to teach two. In second grade I had ample time to provide self-instruction and discovery through learning centers. These are areas consisting of tables, chairs, materials, and activities that children may use independently and in small groups. I also had time to teach holistically. Would I be able to do this in first grade? I began to feel the pressure.

My main concern for the first graders was teaching these children how to read. The first day of the school year I decided to see what the class knew. I found that indeed some of these children did not know all the letters of the alphabet. I knew I had my work cut out for me. The first few weeks of school involved reviewing letters and sounds. A routine was developed in which the class spent the first 15 minutes of each day learning letter sounds. In this phonics activity the children brought in an object to share that began with the letter of the day. During this time, I tried to explain to my children the importance of learning sounds and rules; I wanted my children to become independent readers. I wanted them to use phonics as a tool to help them decode words, but I wanted them to know and use graphemic and other word recognition strategies as well.

After the phonics lesson, the children shared their objects. Next, we wrote our "daily news," telling what each person brought. After the daily news was recorded, I read what the children had dictated, and then we all read it together several times. Finally, I asked for volunteers to read the daily news. Surprisingly, the students were able to read what we had written. Consequently, the daily news activity was helping my children learn to read. Through this simple writing lesson the children were not only learning words, they were also learning sentence structure, punctuation, and capitalization rules.

Following the daily news activity I spent 15 minutes reading to the class. I usually read stories about the unit being studied. After reading the stories, we discussed what we had learned and recorded this in our daily news. Next, the class read the daily news together. We also used the daily news to reinforce what we had discussed in our strategy lessons, and we circled new words we had learned. Once or twice a week we would make a bar graph using words that appeared often in our daily news. The children would look for words that were used more than once and circle those words in different colors. Tally marks were used to count how many times the circled words appeared, then this information was used to create the graph. This word recognition strategy not only allowed the students to see what words were used frequently, but also reinforced their math skills.

After our morning phonics lesson, story, and daily news, the children participated in learning centers. One center was a basal center in which we used our district's adopted series. Although many teachers do not like using basal readers, I have found, especially for those children who do not have many books at home, the basal reader provides an anthology of interesting and appropriate literature and an opportunity to practice reading at a grade-appropriate reading level.

Because writing is an important part of balanced literacy instruction, I also developed a writing center. In the writing area the children wrote stories about the unit they were studying. This provided opportunities for them to think critically and creatively about the subject and to add to their graphemic knowledge and comprehension.

The third center was the library center. Students could choose a book and respond to the book through art or writing, again adding to the development of creativity and critical thinking skills and knowledge of sentence structure, punctuation, and grammar. The books provided for their selection pertained to the unit being studied.

The fourth center varied each week. Sometimes games were used to reinforce skills and other times art activities were provided to complement the unit being studied. Children in this center also listened to Marie Carbo tape-recorded books and worked on comprehension activities that went along with the tapes. During center time, my assistant and I monitored the students to make sure they were on task. I also used this time to check student progress. I held conferences with individual children and assessed their oral reading skills and comprehension skills using miscue analysis. The students' center assignments were put in their portfolios and checked off on a checklist as they completed them. This allowed me to see if students were accomplishing the required objectives.

After the first few weeks of school, most of the children were able to read some of the stories in the basal reader as well as some easy trade books. Several parents called me and said they could not believe their children were already reading. One parent was especially impressed by her son's reading progress. She said, "Hearing him read for the first time brought tears to my eyes." Another parent said she called several family members to tell them, "Kiedran can read!"

I continued to see progress throughout the school year. When we finished one unit we immediately began another one using the same strategies. The children were able to recognize letters and sounds of letters and read for meaning. Their writing improved. They began to write in complete sentences and to use some conventional spelling. The children took advantage of the many opportunities I provided for reading books of their choice. Many of the parents were very supportive of my efforts to teach the children to read. They helped the children at home by listening to them read and by reading aloud to them.

At the end of the year I wanted to find out exactly how my children felt about reading and how they thought they had progressed throughout the year. Using the daily news format each child responded in the following manner:

Daily News 9:30 a.m.

Cassie said, "Today is May 23, 1997." Kiedran said, "I learned to read by reading the daily news." Shannon said, "I like to sound out new words." Jared said, "I am a good reader and I like to read books about space." Nick said, "I can read second-grade words!" Debbie said, "I like to read to my mama and daddy." Terry said, "Reading is important to me because it helps me learn new things." Quincee said, "I didn't know how to read in kindergarten." Kim said, "I learned to read by following along as people read to me." Tanya said, "I couldn't read before I came to first grade but now I can!" Becky said, "I learn new words by sounding them out." James said, "Reading is fun, fun, fun!"

I must say my first year as a first-grade teacher was a success. I found that a few students were phonetic learners and needed the phonics lesson I presented each morning. I also had some students who learned best through sight-word recognition; those children benefited from the daily news and from language experience stories. It became obvious that in order to meet the needs of each student and create a successful reading program, I had to present a balance between phonics and whole language. Basing my instruction on research (for example, Adams, 1990; Goodman, 1990; Manzo & Manzo, 1995; Thompson, 1997) helped me to find the reading method to meet the needs of my students.

Concluding Thoughts

Beginning reading instruction is critical to a child's success in school and throughout his or her life. Effective teachers must be aware of research and best practices in the teaching of reading. In her first year of teaching first-grade reading, Beth used a research-based, balanced approach and combined components from the literature, phonics, and writing approaches to teach reading to her students. By using a balanced approach she was able to meet the needs of a diverse group of students. All the children benefited from different instructional components such as writing, oral language development, reading to the children, and continuous monitoring and assessment. Beth's support for her students at such a critical time in their academic lives provided a strong foundation for a love of reading and future academic achievement. Balanced instruction was the key to this support.

REFERENCES

Adams, M.J. (1990). *Beginning to read: Thinking and learning about print*. Cambridge, MA: Massachusetts Institute of Technology Press.

Burns, P.C., Roe, B.D., & Ross, E.P. (1999). *Teaching reading in today's elementary schools* (7th ed.). Boston, MA: Houghton Mifflin.

Carbo, M. (1996a). Whole language vs. phonics: The great debate. *Principal, 75,* 36–38.

Carbo, M. (1996b). Whole language or phonics? Use both! *Education Digest, 61*(6), 60–65.

Diegmueller, K. (1996). The best of both worlds. *Teacher Magazine, 7*(8), 23–23.

Foorman, B.R., Frances, D.J., Navy, D.M., & Lebirman, D. (1991). How letter-sound instruction mediates progress in first-grade reading and spelling. *Journal of Psychology, 83,* 459–469.

Goodman, Y.M. (1990). *Kid watching: An alternative to testing* (6th ed.). New York: Macmillan.

Heilman, A.W., Blair, T.R., & Rupley, W.H. (1998). *Principles and practices of teaching reading*. New York: Merrill.

Honig, B. (1997). Reading the right way. *The School Administrator, 54*(8), 5–6

Maggart, Z.R., & Zintz, M.V. (1992). *Reading process: The teacher and the learner*. New York: William C. Brown.

Manzo, A.V., & Manzo, U.C. (1995). *Teaching children to be literate: A reflective approach*. New York: Harcourt Brace.

May, F.B. (1998). *Reading as communication—To help children read and write* (5th ed.). Columbus, OH: Merrill.

Morgan, K.B. (1995). Creative phonics: A meaning-oriented reading program. *Intervention in School and Clinic, 30*(5), 287–291.

Morrow, L.M., & Tracey, D.H. (1997). Strategies used for phonics instruction in early childhood classrooms. *The Reading Teacher, 50*, 80, 644–651.

Pikulski, J.J. (1997, October/November). Beginning reading instruction: From "The great debate" to the reading wars. *Reading Today*, p. 32.

Richgels, D.J., Poremba, K.J., & McGee, L.M. (1996). Kindergartners talk about print: Phonemic awareness in meaningful contexts. *The Reading Teacher, 49*(8), 632–641.

Smith, M.S., Stevenson, D.L., & Li, C.P. (1998). Voluntary national tests: Helping schools improve instruction and learning in reading and mathematics. *Phi Delta Kappan, 80*(3), 213–218.

Stanovich, K.E. (1986). Matthew effects in reading: Some consequences of individual differences in the acquisition of literacy. *Reading Research Quarterly, 21*(4), 360–407.

Strickland, D. (1998). Balanced literacy: Teaching the skills and thrills of reading. *Instructor* [Online]. Available: www.scholastic.com/instructor/curriculum/langarts/reading/balanced.htm

Thompson, R. (1997). The philosophy of balanced reading instruction. *The Journal of Balanced Reading Instruction, 4*(D1), 28–29.

U.S. Department of Education. (1998). *The Reading Summit* [Online]. Available: www.ed.gov/inits/readingsummit/

Weaver, C. (1998). *Phonics in whole language classrooms* [Online]. Available: www.kidsource.com/kidsource/content2/phonics.html

White, B. (1996, May 27). Reading—A new chapter. *The Atlanta Journal Constitution*, p. D6–D7.

CHAPTER 7

Implementing a Balanced Beginning Reading Program in Culturally and Linguistically Diverse Classrooms

Jan E. Hasbrouck and Milly Schrader

There is strong research support for developing and implementing balanced reading programs for beginning readers. Programs that strike a balance between skills activities and authentic, purposeful literacy activities appear to be the best for children who are learning to read and write. Teachers and administrators who have heard and embraced this clear and hopeful message are left to wonder how to develop a program with appropriate, reasonable, and effective balance and how to implement such a program in real-world classrooms. For those educators responsible for teaching children from culturally and linguistically diverse backgrounds, the question of how to implement a balanced program becomes even more challenging.

This chapter presents the story of one northern California elementary school, Herman Leimbach Elementary, and its successful implementation of a balanced reading program in its first-grade classrooms. We begin by describing how the program was developed and recalling the first year in which this program was implemented. This is the story of a real school, in a real community, with the same real problems and issues facing many schools today. This is a school in which the administrators, teachers, and parents worked together to develop and implement an effective program for its beginning readers.

School Profile

Herman Leimbach Elementary is a large school serving more than 900 children in grades K–6. The classroom enrollments are also large. During the first year of this project 33 students were taught in the kindergarten classrooms, 32 in all first-, second-, and third-grade classrooms, and 34 in each of the upper-elementary classes. The school is located in the rapidly growing suburban community of Elk Grove, located just south of Sacramento, California. This community, like many in this and other states, has seen a dramatic growth in the number of families of newly arrived immigrants from around the world. At the time this balanced program was implemented, Elk Grove School District served students who spoke more than 50 different languages at home; Leimbach alone served students who spoke more than 20 different languages. Along with these children from immigrant families, Leimbach also served children from lower and middle socioeconomic status white, African American, Asian, and Hispanic families.

To help address the vast range of needs of such a diverse group of children, Leimbach had two language development classrooms (one for primary-grade students and one for upper-grade students), to serve students with non–English proficiency (NEP) or limited–English proficiency (LEP). The school also had two full-time special education teachers (each with a part-time instructional assistant), a Title I coordinator, a Title I teacher with seven part-time instructional assistants, and a part-time parent/community liaison.

Making Changes From the Top Down and Bottom Up

Milly Schrader, the second author of this chapter, was the principal of Leimbach and had been deeply concerned about the performance of primary-grade students on the annual standardized reading assessments conducted by the school district. For several years before this project began, Leimbach students had ranked well below the district average in reading. This resulted in the school's being categorized as a low-performing target school in the district.

Milly wanted to address the "at-risk" status of Leimbach. She believed that, at least in part, this was why the district had hired her and assigned her to this challenging school. Her background in working with school improvement and curriculum development gave her a wealth of skills that could help make important changes and improvements in a school such as Leimbach.

Milly knew that improving her school's "target school" classification would require making changes in how Leimbach students were being instructed in reading and related language arts. As an experienced instructional leader, she also knew that changing the status quo in school procedures can be a very difficult thing to accomplish, but that a plan for making improvements would have a better chance of being embraced and implemented by her teachers if they were invested in the plan and its intended outcomes.

In this case Milly decided to proceed with a change process that involved components that were both "top-down" (decisions made by her alone) and "bottom-up" (decisions made with input from the participating teachers). In order to maximize the available resources and efforts, she unilaterally decided to focus on the reading program in the first-grade classrooms only. She based this "top-down" decision on two reasons. One reason was that current research on reading supported the critical importance of effective beginning reading instruction to provide a foundation for all future learning (Adams, 1990; McPartland & Slavin, 1990; Snow, Burns, & Griffin, 1998). Her second reason was based on intangible political factors with which school administrators must grapple continually. Although she would have liked to target her kindergarten, first-grade, and second-grade programs, Milly believed that she would have more support and cooperation from the first-grade teachers. Her hope was that *if* a successful program could be implemented in the first-grade classrooms and teachers could see the improved skill levels of the first-grade students, that teachers in the kindergarten and then the second-grade classrooms would be more willing to make changes in their own programs.

After making this initial decision, Milly embarked on the "bottom-up" part of the plan. She was well informed on the components of an effective reading instructional program. She wanted her teachers to develop and implement a more balanced instructional program than the primarily whole language and literature-based program currently in place. Although she is an experienced curriculum and program developer, Milly did not want decisions made at this step of the process to be made by her alone. She knew that some of the first-grade teachers would need some convincing to make changes in their program, and that Milly's efforts as the school principal could be perceived as unwanted pressure or coercion. Because Milly also wanted to maintain a positive and supportive professional relationship with her teachers, she decided to use an outside consultant to help with this key step in the process.

The first author of this chapter, Jan Hasbrouck, was working as a private educational consultant at the time of this project. She was brought in at this early stage to meet with the first-grade teachers; to share findings from empirical research, field-based implementations, and program evaluations; and to help them decide in which direction they would like to proceed to make improvements in their language arts program.

Planning a Balanced Instructional Program

The group of teachers involved in developing this new plan reflected the diversity of the students they taught in their own cultural backgrounds, levels of experience, and original training. The most experienced teacher in the group, with more than 20 years in the classroom, was Joyce Lum, a Chinese American. She had begun her own school experience as a non–English-speaking student who at times had been placed in the closet of her kindergarten classroom for not speaking English correctly. Diana Sandoval, who had 5 years of teaching experience, was Hispanic and very proud and respectful of her cultural heritage. The two other teachers were both white. Patricia Webb had been trained as a special educator and had 15 years teaching experience, mostly at the junior high level and with very challenging students identified as academically and behaviorally at risk. Maurine Smith was a beginning teacher with just 2 years' experience teaching in first grade. The teacher of the primary language development classroom, Ann Go, had been teaching for 5 years. She had emigrated to the United States from Vietnam as a teenager and spoke Vietnamese and Chinese in addition to English.

The teachers from this group with the least experience expressed the greatest frustration with the lack of progress they had seen in their students. They had been trained in whole language and literature-based instructional methodologies in their teacher preparation courses, and had tried very hard to use those strategies effectively with their students with high hopes for success. When the majority of their students were leaving first grade without reading or writing at acceptable levels, they felt at a loss as to the best way to proceed.

One of the more experienced teachers had generally been having success with the majority of her students in recent years and was therefore the most reluctant participant in this change process. Although like her fellow teachers she used the district curriculum as the basis for her instruction, over the years she had pieced together an eclectic program, balancing decoding skills instruction, reading connected text, comprehension instruction, and motivational activities to achieve a generally high rate of success with most of her students. However, she expressed a strong desire to follow whatever decision her colleagues made regarding a new instructional plan for reading. She wanted to be part of the group, not in her words, a "rebel outsider."

Jan conducted a series of after-school meetings and staff presentations in the spring of the year before this project was first implemented with the four first-grade teachers and the primary language development classroom teacher, with input from the Title I teachers. The teachers all freely expressed to Jan their personal frustrations with their students' reading skills. They complained about the level of readiness with which their students entered the first grade as well as the effectiveness of their current curriculum materials. They were generally pleased that Milly wanted to address the status of Leimbach as an at-risk school, but they were somewhat confused about what changes should be made, and apprehensive about what a new program would mean to them and the procedures they were comfortable using in their individual classrooms.

One of the teachers' issues appeared to be concern about the level of accountability a new program might initiate. She was worried that a program with clear standards or performance benchmarks would hold the teachers to a high performance standard. The teachers were aware that their students were not currently achieving acceptable skill levels in reading, but the program goals were not defined clearly, so there were no accompanying repercussions or criticisms of the instruction. A new program might change that.

Milly encouraged the teachers to look at successful programs currently implemented in other schools. She hired substitute teachers to allow the Leimbach teachers to have time away from their classrooms to visit other sites. Continuing the top-down/bottom-up implementation process, Milly suggested two schools to visit and let the teachers pick others. In all, the teachers visited between four and five schools to observe a variety of programs.

Jan began the planning process by listening to the teachers' concerns and then sharing findings from research and from her own experience working with low-performing children as a reading specialist and administrator. Results from studies and field implementations of programs representing the best of skills-oriented instructional procedures as well as whole language, literature-based programs were presented and discussed. The conclusions of Adams in her book *Learning to Read: Thinking and Learning About Print* (1990) were especially helpful. The idea of developing and implementing a balanced program was appealing to the teachers. They accepted the rationale and noted the obvious weaknesses in their current program.

An ideal balanced reading program would integrate, within a single instructional model, the empirically supported processing and comprehension skills and the motivational aspects of learning to read, and the program would be implemented individually for each child. Given the limited time, money, and specialized training available to this school, the political climate mandating quick results, the requirement to continue use of the district curriculum, and the widely diverse nature of the children, the team decided to achieve a balance in their reading program by finding components that could be used in a coordinated and responsive fashion to increase their students' reading achievement. Together, with input from Milly, the Title I teachers, the teachers, and Jan, the group developed a balanced program they decided to try.

Given the strong research support for the effectiveness of direct instruction programs for students with low levels of readiness to read and those identified as at risk and low performing, the group decided to use these types of materials as the cornerstone of the "skills" part of their new program. They selected the Science Research Associates (SRA) reading mastery program (RM) and the B.E.S.T. introductory phonics program (BEST) (Dougall, Hasbrouck, & Austin, 1982/1999). Both programs provided explicit instruction in phonics, phonemic awareness, and beginning decoding skills (such as left-to-right tracking, blending, and sentence reading). RM was targeted to be used with the lowest skilled students because it was the most highly structured and comprehensive program available. Because BEST was shorter and presented skills at a more rapid pace, it was to be used with those students who demonstrated some understanding of beginning reading skills and a moderate level of readiness at the start of the year. The teachers also decided to use the SRA reasoning and writing program to provide direct instruction in comprehension and writing skills.

The balance to this skills emphasis in their program was to be provided by the district curriculum, the Houghton Mifflin Literacy Readers, a literature-based reading series. The teachers' own wealth of training in whole language, writing process procedures, and other enriching, motivating methods would complete the new program.

Dealing With District Politics

The reality of schools usually involves some amount of dealing with political policies and practices, and this project was no different. The district had targeted Leimbach as a below-average school. To Milly, this label was an indication that current practice at the school was inadequate and changes needed to be made. Thus, there was some expectation that the district would enthusiastically support a thoughtful, empirically founded improvement plan.

At the conclusion of the series of meetings with Jan and teachers in the spring, Milly approached district representatives, including the administrator who served as both the Director of Staff Development and the Reading Specialist Coordinator, with the new reading plan for Leimbach. The district coordinator was only mildly supportive. She reminded Milly that (then) the California State Frameworks for Reading required the use of a literature-based program for reading instruction in classrooms and that this new plan appeared to deviate from the use of the mandated core curriculum. The coordinator also expressed lack of enthusiasm for direct instruction programs, even though Milly presented evidence of the supportive research on its effectiveness. Milly persisted, holding numerous discussions with district-level administrators, and ultimately received approval to implement the program for one year. All financial and personnel support for the project was provided by the school's budget that first year.

Milly believed that the implementation of the program was simply tolerated, rather than supported enthusiastically by the district. The district administrators were not invested in the success of the program: If the program succeeded, great; if not, there would be no negative consequences for them. In retrospect, Milly now sees some benefit to this initial lack of enthusiasm by her supervisors because it gave her a certain amount of freedom from scrutiny. She was able to implement the project using her own goals, standards, and procedures, rather than ones imposed by others. The district also did not dictate any criteria for evaluating the success of this program, leaving the principal to define her own criteria: successful student performance in reading and language arts on the Comprehensive Test of Basic Skills (CTBS) (1991), a widely used comprehensive standardized achievement test.

Getting Started: Implementing the Program

In September of the following school year, a team of instructional assistants and teachers individually screened all 130 first-grade students for their knowledge of names and common sounds of isolated upper- and lowercase letters; their ability to read selected preprimer- and primer-level words from the Dolch word list, a frequently used graded list of common sight words; and their ability to decode a list of 10 phonically regular three- and four-letter words (CVC, CCVC, and CVCC). Had a student been able to correctly identify these sounds, letters, and words, he or she would have been asked to read from two stories selected from the classroom readers. However, none of the students demonstrated skills at this level. Students' expressive and receptive language skills were assessed informally using the pretest of the Distar Language I curriculum (SRA, 1987). Informal observations of students' writing skills were made in the classrooms by their teachers.

Screening Results

Students' performances on the reading assessments were categorized into one of five groups. Those students who

5. correctly identified 100% of letter names and sounds; confidently and accurately decoded the CVC, CVCC, and CCVC words as well as some irregular words (less than 3 seconds per correctly read word; fewer than 2 errors). Language skills strong (fewer than 3 errors on the language screener).

4. correctly identified 100% of letter names and sounds; successfully decoded some of the regular CVC words (3 to 5 seconds per correctly read word; at least 3 of the 10 words correctly decoded). Language skills strong.

3. correctly identified 100% of letter names and sounds; sounds not accurately blended to decode words. Language skills moderate to strong (3 to 5 errors on the language screener).

2. know most letter names but cannot identify them confidently; letter sounds unknown or very weak. Language skills moderate to weak (over 5 errors on the language screener).

1. know few or no letter names or sounds. Language skills moderate to weak.

Only one first grader out of 130 tested was found to fit the criteria of category 5. Her mother chose to remove her from the school during the first month and enroll her in a private school. Score summaries from 56 students' (43%) skills matched categories 4 and 3. The remaining students were considered at risk for academic difficulty in reading and were referred for assistance from Title I.

Grouping for Instruction

The lowest performing students in each classroom received instruction from RM materials while all others were taught from the more rapidly paced BEST materials. Students with extremely limited proficiency in English were placed in the intensive language development classroom and received daily lessons from the BEST and RM programs while developing skills in English. Throughout the year, students from the language development classroom moved into the traditional first-grade classrooms when the teacher determined their receptive and expressive English had reached acceptable levels of proficiency.

First-grade students who qualified for Title I received assistance within their regular classrooms using the same programs as their classmates. Title I funds were used to hire instructional assistants to work alongside the classroom teachers to provide intensive, small-group instruction in extended day programs to identified students. The regular school day for Leimbach first graders was 9:00 a.m. to 1:50 p.m. Some of the Title I students came at 8:00 a.m. and left at the end of the regular day while others arrived at 9:00 a.m. and stayed until 2:40 p.m. This extended instruction was supplemental to students' regular lessons that were taught during the daily 2½-hour language arts/reading block. This extended time was used exclusively either to preteach or reteach the day's lesson. If students demonstrated proficiency in the day's skill, the time was used for extension activities directly related to that day's lesson.

Addressing Cultural and Linguistic Diversity

The staff and administration of Leimbach were very committed to honoring and supporting the cultural diversity of the students attending their school. There were many forums encouraging active parent involvement. The parent group worked closely with the Leimbach administrators to develop a plan to bring the diversity of the community into the school. Each month of the school year the entire school celebrated one of the major cultural groups represented by Leimbach families. During the month, special meals were served by the school cafeteria and talent shows were held to showcase the dance, music, games, and other practices of the featured culture. Teachers also planned special activities in each classroom to encourage respect and appreciation for each individual child and his or her family.

However, the diversity of languages spoken in Leimbach students' homes could not be addressed through bilingual instruction, teaching the NEP or LEP students to read in their native language. There were simply not enough resources to support this model of instruction. Also, the parents of Leimbach's NEP/LEP students were clear in their goals for their children's literacy development: They wanted their children to learn to speak, read, and write effectively in English in order to succeed in the educational system in the United States. These parents believed it was their job, however, to maintain and support their children's first language and native culture.

This model seemed to work well. It was fascinating for us to watch the NEP/LEP students in the language development classroom learning to decode their English stories with steadily increasing accuracy and fluency while at the same time learning to speak and understand English. At different times during the year, students' English proficiency caught up with their decoding proficiency. These students often became very excited when they suddenly could comprehend the stories they had been decoding. They frequently would want to re-read the stories they had "read" previously with little or no comprehension. We did not keep any separate data on the performance of the students in this classroom, but our informal observations convinced us that these students were acquiring reading and writing skills in their second language at a reasonable rate and with good proficiency.

How the Program Worked During the First Year

This project took place in a real-world environment, not in a clinically controlled setting. Although the team of teachers charged with developing this new instructional program took their task seriously and were in agreement about the need for balance in their students' literacy instruction, in actual implementation the classrooms involved were not identical to one another.

Each of the teachers involved in this project had her own instructional style, individual level of commitment to the goals of the project, and level of expertise. All varied in their philosophical beliefs about teaching, and these differences could be seen in their classroom set-ups and structures; one teacher ran a highly structured teacher-directed classroom where basic skills were emphasized, while the students in the classroom next door spent much of their day engaged in "free-choice" activities in a less structured environment. All teachers used the agreed-on combination of direct instruction and whole language/literature-based instruction with their students, but each interpreted and implemented this new balanced program in her own manner and made it work for students in different ways.

One guideline developed for the new program was that all instructional groups be flexible and reorganized continuously throughout the year as necessary. This decision was made to avoid one of the biggest criticisms of ability grouping: students locked forever in the lowest group, receiving the poorest quality instruction (Flood, Lapp, Flood, & Nagel, 1992; Lou et al., 1996; Slavin, 1987). Because both BEST and RM have weekly assessments built into their programs, teachers had relevant data available for making decisions about regrouping. At the end of the project year the Leimbach teachers agreed that this guideline had been followed easily and successfully.

The skills instruction was carried out in small homogenous ability groups that met daily for approximately 25 minutes, while writing and literature activities were conducted as large-group lessons with all students in each classroom working and learning together. The classrooms involved in the project were literate environments (Goodman, 1986) filled with books, newspapers, magazines, posters, and environmental print. Students in each class were given frequent opportunities each week to experiment with authentic and highly motivating ways to use their emerging literacy skills by writing, illustrating, and publishing their own books and newsletters, writing group and individual letters, and other activities. Students shared their favorite literature with classmates through dramatic readings and puppet shows.

The teachers used the primers and first-grade reader from the district-adopted series. Books from the district's required reading list along with other trade books from each teacher's classroom library or the school library also were used to provide the students with a background in high-quality literature. Teachers read aloud to their students daily from these materials and children often took these materials home to share. The children learned repetitive sections of predictable stories and chorally read these parts aloud from their own individual books. As their reading skills progressed during the school year, the first graders were encouraged to read from these and other books independently and did so with increasing frequency.

Writing also was emphasized strongly by all the teachers. Meaningful writing and spelling activities incorporating phonics skills promoted the reading/writing connection. Teachers used daily journal writing, writing process instruction, author's chairs, whole-class poetry writing, and other techniques to encourage students to become confident, skillful, and proficient writers. Each classroom developed over time a heavily used library of student authored, illustrated, and published books.

A key goal of this plan, insisted on by district-level administrators and agreed on by the Leimbach teachers and Milly, was to move students into the district's adopted reading curriculum as soon as they demonstrated they could be successful with those materials. All teachers complied with this request. At various times throughout the school year, students receiving instruction from BEST or RM were transitioned into the standard first-grade materials.

Evaluation of the Students' Reading

Milly and participating teachers were eager to find ways to evaluate the effects of their redesigned program. The principal of Washington Elementary (pseudonym), located within the same district, was asked if the first-grade classes at her school could be used as a comparison group in an informal evaluation. Washington was targeted because it shares many characteristics with Leimbach. Class sizes are very large in both schools and students are highly diverse racially, culturally, and linguistically, and come from low socioeconomic status homes and have high mobility. Like Leimbach, Washington had been identified by the district as at risk because of several years of consistently low scores on the achievement test administered annually to all students in the district. Washington teachers used the district's adopted literature-based program and whole language procedures as their reading curriculum in their first-grade classrooms. Washington's principal agreed to ask her first-grade teachers if they would be willing participants in the evaluation. Two of the four teachers expressed a desire to participate.

Results From Standardized Achievement Testing

The CTBS was administered in the spring of the project year to all students in the district. This included both the students who had been attending Leimbach all year and had received a full year of the new balanced program, and those who had moved into the school from January until the time of the test administration. The average reading performance (based on the total reading battery of the CTBS) of all first graders in the district during the project year was at the 41st percentile of national norms. Leimbach's first-grade students' reading scores placed them at the 52nd percentile. The previous year's first graders at Leimbach had scored at the 40th percentile on the same test. This was the first time Leimbach students had ever performed above the district average, so these results were considered a major improvement. Washington's first graders placed at the 28th percentile while their previous year's first graders had placed at the 46th percentile.

Results From Informal Reading Assessments

The Leimbach teachers and administrator wanted additional information about the effects of the new program on their students' reading abilities besides the results from the CTBS assessments. All the teachers agreed that one important piece of evidence of reading proficiency is the ability of a child to accurately and fluently decode an unpracticed passage at his or her grade level. With limited time and trained personnel available, a small-scale evaluation was designed that involved this kind of assessment. It was decided an oral reading fluency (ORF) test would be used to assess each student. ORF was selected because it is a naturalistic activity that has been shown in numerous studies to be technically adequate (Hasbrouck & Tindal, 1992) and highly related to other important reading skills, including comprehension (Adams, 1990).

In ORF tasks, students orally read one or more samples of grade-level materials for one-minute periods. The total number of words read by the student in one minute is used as the base score and the number of errors subtracted from this amount. Errors include omissions and substitutions or mispronunciations. If a student has not successfully read a word after three seconds the word is supplied by the examiner and counted as an error. Inserted words or errors that were self-corrected by the student are not counted as errors. The final score is the number of words correct per minute (wcpm) (Shinn, 1989).

Teachers in the first-grade classrooms at Leimbach and Washington were asked to select students with high, average, and lower level reading skills, five or six students representing each level. This stratified sample of 47 students from each of the four general education first-grade classrooms at Leimbach and 21 students from two classrooms at Washington were individually assessed in February and again in May. For both assessments, students orally read from two passages for one minute each. One passage was a literature-based story while the other was a phonically regular passage with a controlled vocabulary. These types of passages were selected to avoid a bias for or against students receiving different types of instructional programs. A total of four different stories were used in the two assessment periods. The passages had not been read previously by the students and were read with no prior practice following a brief introduction of story by the examiner.

In late February, the average oral reading scores from the sample of students at Leimbach was 27 wcpm with 6 errors; the average from the two Washington classrooms was 20 wcpm with 10 errors. Leimbach students were reading correctly approximately 35% more words with almost half the errors on identical tasks. In May, students in both programs had improved. However, Leimbach students' average was 51 wcpm with five errors (an improvement of 24 wcpm) while the Washington students' average was 36 wcpm with seven errors. Leimbach's first graders had gained 24 wcpm in 3 months as opposed to a gain of 16 wcpm for Washington's students.

Although no national performance norms for ORF for first grade are currently available, a goal for first graders' orally reading unpracticed stories is typically in the range of 60 wcpm with fewer than five errors by the end of first grade (Carnine, Silbert, & Kameenui, 1996). Forty-six percent of the tested students from Leimbach met the criterion while only four of the 21 Washington students (19%) were at this level.

Interpreting these results in terms of growth is somewhat problematic because no data were available on the initial reading levels of the students from Washington. The screening of the Leimbach students at the start of the year found that none were reading words in sentences at that time. Although 43% of Leimbach's students accurately identified the common sounds of letters in the initial screening, only a few were able to decode phonically regular three-letter words. By teacher report, two of the Washington students tested in this evaluation had entered first grade already reading fluently. Simply examining the final scores, however, does show a notable difference in performance between students in the two programs, both on the CTBS and ORF assessments. By the end of first grade, only four of the 21 Washington students could read unpracticed first-grade materials with reasonable independence (60 wcpm with at least 92% accuracy) while nearly half of the assessed Leimbach students had achieved this skill level. (See Chapter 5 for further discussion on assessing literacy learners.)

Special Education Referrals

One indication that a beginning reading program is effective can be measured by how many students are referred for special education. The year before this project was implemented at Leimbach, 117 referrals were submitted for special education assessments from the 10 first- and second-grade classrooms. The first year after this project, only 9 re-

---

ferrals were submitted, and only 11 were submitted the second year. This dramatic change in referrals indicates not only that larger numbers of students were succeeding in acquiring reading and writing skills, but also that teachers felt empowered to deal with lower performing students in their own classrooms because they now had effective tools and instructional strategies. This reduced dependence on special education also had the effect of freeing the special education teachers to focus their efforts on the most needy children.

Anecdotal Evaluation

Of course, assessment scores can only tell part of the story of this project. Teachers and parents from Leimbach reported a dramatic improvement in students' reading, writing, and spelling compared to prior years. Two parents with children in both first- and second-grade classes at Leimbach reported to the principal that their first-grade children were more skillful and confident readers than their older siblings. As part of a school-wide writing assessment, the sixth-grade teachers were given first graders' papers to score holistically. They initially refused to believe that the samples had been written by first graders because the stories were so long and so well written. Two of Leimbach's first-grade teachers noted that children from their classes frequently asked to stay in class during recess to finish writing poems or stories and that this positive attitude about reading and writing was very different from previous years.

Milly shared these evaluation results with the district administrators. Based on these positive findings, the district continued to support the project at the same level for the next year, even though the project did not use the district core curriculum. Over the next few years, the principal found resources to extend the direct instruction component into the second and third grades to complement and balance the existing literature-based program. Continued assessment results across the next 4 years showed that students who received the balanced direct instruction/literature-based program in the first three grades out-performed their district peers in reading comprehension each year and continued to do so through fourth grade. However, these students fell below their peers in reading comprehension performance by the fifth grade. Milly used these results to convince the district to provide direct instruction materials in grades 4, 5, and 6.

Conclusion

The teachers at Herman Leimbach Elementary are faced with the same challenge as many other schools today: how to teach culturally diverse, transient, and economically disadvantaged children to learn to read and write successfully with limited resources. Their response to this increasingly common concern was to design and implement a program that systematically combined the proven power of explicit instruction in decoding skills with exciting and highly motivating whole language, literature-based procedures. Milly used a combination of results from published research and assessment data from her own students to build a case with the district's administrators for helping develop an effective balanced program.

The experience of the teachers, parents, and administrators of Leimbach provides an example of how one school designed and implemented a balanced instructional program. Importantly, evaluation evidence confirmed that this type of program is indeed effective, in a real school, with real children, with real problems and challenges.

REFERENCES

Adams, M.J. (1990). *Beginning to read: Thinking and learning about print.* Cambridge, MA: Massachusetts Institute of Technology Press.

Carnine, D., Silbert, J., & Kameenui, E.J. (1996). *Direct instruction reading.* Columbus, OH: Merrill.

Comprehensive Test of Basic Skills. (1991). Monterey, CA: Comprehensive test of basic skills/McGraw-Hill.

Dougall, J., Hasbrouck, J., & Austin, J. (1982/1999). *The B.E.S.T. introductory phonics program.* Springfield, OR: B.E.S.T. Publications.

Flood, J., Lapp, D., Flood, S., & Nagal, G. (1992). Am I allowed to group? Using flexible patterns for effective instruction. *The Reading Teacher, 45*(8), 608–616.

Goodman, K. (1986). *What's whole in whole language?* Portsmouth, NH: Heinemann.

Hasbrouck, J.E., & Tindal, G. (1992). Curriculum-based oral reading fluency norms for students in grades 2 through 5. *Teaching Exceptional Children, 24*(3), 41–44.

Lou, Y., Abrami, P.C., Spence, J.C., Poulsen, C., Chambers, B., & d'Apollonia, S. (1996). Within-class grouping: A meta-analysis. *Review of Educational Research, 66*(4), 423-458.

McPartland, J.M., & Slavin, R.E. (1990). *Policy perspectives: Increasing achievement of at-risk students at each grade level.* Washington, DC: U.S. Department of Education, Office of Research and Improvement.

Science Research Associates. (1987). *Distar Language I.* Chicago, IL: Author.

Science Research Associates. (1994). *Reading Mastery.* Chicago, IL: Author

Shinn, M.R. (1989). *Curriculum-based measurement: Assessing special children.* New York: Guilford.

Slavin, R.E. (1987). Ability grouping and student achievement in elementary schools: A best evidence synthesis. *Review of Educational Research, 57*(3), 293–336.

Snow, C.E., Burns, M.S., & Griffin, P. (1998). *Preventing reading difficulties in young children.* Washington, DC: National Academy Press.

Vaughn, S., Moody, S.W., & Schumm, J.S. (1998). Broken promises: Reading instruction in the resource room. *Exceptional Children, 64*(2), 211–225.

CHAPTER 8

Balanced Literacy Instruction in the Elementary School: The West Hanover Story

Barbara A. Marinak and William A. Henk

During the 1990s, West Hanover Elementary School successfully engineered a quiet literacy revolution. The teachers immersed themselves in the professional literature, engaged in intensive problem solving, avoided politics, and built community trust, all in an effort to maximize literacy learning for students. The journey did not begin as a search for what the literature now calls "balanced literacy instruction" (Freppon & Dahl, 1998). Rather, it was an attempt to construct an effective whole language framework for our elementary students. Because there did not appear to be a consistent definition of whole language in these early days, it was necessary to identify areas for change. Specifically, we wanted to move away from basal readers that were too constraining, groups that were overly confining, and workbooks that lacked purpose. We believed that with a strong theoretical framework, highly knowledgeable teachers, and a commitment to authentic literacy experiences, our school could redefine grade-level expectations and help children become motivated readers and writers. Along the way, we found balance.

Experience told us that certain "traditional" literacy practices were absolutely necessary for children to grow as readers and writers. Working with words and daily exposure to the sounds of the language were among the more conventional practices we were sure to keep. Savviness taught us to learn from the mistakes of others. We knew from various sources that flexible grouping was essential, and we confirmed rather quickly that reading cannot be taught with single copies of trade titles. Finally, courage allowed us take calculated risks: Portfolios became more informative than workbook pages and student choice was recognized as a powerful motivator.

What began as a simple journey toward effective literacy instruction evolved into a full-blown nomadic adventure. As a result of these travels, we have learned to be patient, confident, and open-minded. We are comfortable with the notion of never arriving at a fixed destination and excited that with each passing year, literacy instruction will look, feel, and sound just a little different than it did the year before.

In this chapter, we describe the balanced instruction that has evolved at West Hanover. The first author (Marinak) served as the reading consultant to West Hanover from 1984 to 1996 and remains responsible for the instructional framework at the school. The second author (Henk), through a partnership between Central Dauphin School District and Penn State-Harrisburg, consulted frequently with the administrative staff as the model was developed. He continues to collaborate with the district's administrators as West Hanover's practices are shared across the district.

We begin by briefly introducing the school and then outlining the basic components of the schoolwide program. These foundational elements include frameworks for achieving word facility, meaning construction, flexible grouping, text selection, and responding to text. Next, we use these elements as a backdrop for specifying how balanced literacy instruction occurs first in grades kindergarten through 2 and then in grades 3 through 6. We conclude with some final thoughts about the essence of the journey and the generalizability of our experiences to other school contexts.

West Hanover Elementary School located in southcentral Pennsylvania is one of 14 elementary schools in a large suburban district of over 11,000 children. The school serves approximately 300 children in kindergarten through grade 6, with three classrooms representing each grade level. Class size ranges from 20 to 22 children in the primary grades to 25 to 28 children in the intermediate grades. West Hanover could be characterized as a middle-class school with little ethnic diversity and a veteran staff. When our literacy reforms began, each teacher in the building had more than 15 years of teaching experience.

Components of Balanced Literacy at West Hanover

Words and Word Parts

The component we call words and word parts at West Hanover consists of direct instruction in spelling-sound relationships and vocabulary development in the primary grades and word study and vocabulary instruction in the intermediate grades.

Beginning reading instruction at West Hanover contains a balance of activities designed to enhance children's word recognition while reading and to improve their spelling during writing. In the intermediate grades, word recognition and phonemic awareness activities give way to instruction in word-study strategies. Strategies to decode multisyllabic words, the use of context clues, and instruction in word origins all emerge in the intermediate grades.

For all grade levels, we adopted three vocabulary goals from the work of Lipson and Wixson (1997):

1. *Teach independent vocabulary learning.* Provide strategies that encourage and assist readers in acquiring vocabulary independently.

2. *Teach concepts important for comprehension.* Directly teach the words necessary for the understanding of complex concepts.

3. *Create an environment that promotes general vocabulary development.* Provide multiple opportunities for readers and writers to encounter and use an ever-growing collection of words.

Words, though important in and of themselves, are most exciting when strung together to entertain, inform, and persuade audiences. From the earliest days in kindergarten through the final months of sixth grade, students at West Hanover learn that word knowledge allows them to construct meaning from all kinds of text. In this way, they develop an appreciation of various genres and begin to understand the power of words in receptive and expressive language.

Constructing Meaning

From kindergarten on, passion for reading develops from the ability to construct and reconstruct meaning from fiction, nonfiction, poetry, periodicals, and a host of other genres. Professional literature told us that children engage in a variety of strategies before, during, and after reading when interacting with these texts (see, for example, Adams, 1990; Allington, 1983; Rosenblatt, 1983). We soon discovered that strategic readers in the primary grades use essentially the same strategies as strategic readers in the upper-elementary grades. Consequently, in order to make text accessible to our emerging readers, it was necessary to identify and teach these strategies in a developmentally appropriate manner. Reader response and text difficulty are the two important differences in the reading program across grade levels. Reading responses grow in both depth and breadth as children proceed toward middle school, and the literature collection offered to older readers is more challenging than the titles used in the primary grades.

At West Hanover, we believe that effective readers use the before, during, and after reading strategies shown in Figure 1 on the next page. We teach our children that before reading, they should anticipate meaning based on their prior knowledge and familiarity with text, create predictions, and anticipate vocabulary they might encounter. During reading, they are encouraged to confirm or adjust their predictions, to

Figure 1
Strategies for Effective Reading

Before Reading
Anticipate meaning
Create predictions
Anticipate vocabulary

During Reading
Confirm or adjust predictions
Construct meaning from fiction
Construct meaning from nonfiction
Monitor meaning while reading
Use fix-up strategies

After Reading
Retell
Summarize
Evaluate

construct meaning from text by using the predictable elements of fiction and nonfiction, to monitor meaning while reading, and to use a variety of "fix-up" strategies if meaning breaks down. After reading, we believe that effective readers should be able to retell, summarize, and evaluate text they have read.

A wide variety of specific methods are used to teach before, during, and after reading strategies. These methods and techniques vary across grade levels. Later in the chapter we present the methods and techniques we have found most successful at West Hanover, organized by grade level.

Flexible Grouping

From the beginning of the initiative at West Hanover, grouping was a topic of frequent discussion. Our observations and reading led us to a number of grouping-related issues.

Prior to the implementation of instructional changes, we visited many "whole language" classrooms in the area. We were struck by the number of classroom teachers who, in practice, were defining "whole language" as "whole-class" reading instruction. From Allington's (1983) research, we knew that lowering the teacher/student ratio was vital, especially for struggling readers. Whole-class instruction certainly seemed at odds with these findings. Likewise, we were aware of Slavin's (1983) grouping research that pointed to the cognitive contributions that could be offered by all members of a heterogeneous group, regardless of reading ability. We also discovered research by Hiebert (1983) that addressed optimal group size for effective reading instruction. Moreover, the work of Deci and his colleagues (Deci, Vallerand, Pelletier, & Ryan, 1991) reminded us that choice is perhaps the most powerful motivator during learning—a notion that is lost when whole-class instruction predominates.

From this exploration of grouping, we felt confident that our classrooms should be grouped flexibly and, when possible, arranged in sizes of three to five children. This goal of group size took on special importance in the primary grades as we attempted to address individual reading needs.

Flexible grouping at West Hanover varies across grade levels. However, in general, it is a balance of mixed-ability and similar-ability groups. Balance is achieved by using both teacher-choice (that is, the teacher places children in a similar ability group based on need) and student-choice (that is, the teacher places children in a group by virtue of their book or project choice) groups.

In the primary grades, teacher-choice groups occur more often to ensure direct, systematic instruction in crucial skills and strategies while children emerge as readers. In the intermediate grades, student-choice groups are more prevalent. However, it is important to note that as readers move through the grades, they actively learn how to choose a book for reading group.

Text Selection

At West Hanover, choosing a book for reading group is very different from choosing a book for self-selected reading. Readers learn that with choice comes responsibility. Responsibility has two parameters: comfort and interest. Children learn to choose a book that can be read "comfortably." The five-finger rule (see Figure 2) is taught to help readers make appropriate choices. Secondly, children learn to choose an interesting title around which they can respond—both orally and in writing.

Reading instruction at West Hanover does not focus on a particular book, and it is not important that children "master" any one story. An understanding of genre (for example, mystery, comedy, historical fiction, nonfiction, or biography) and the strategies to derive meaning from these genres are far more important than comprehending a given title. Repeated experiences through the years with a variety of genres and a consistent core of strategies has served to define reading instruction at the school. By focusing instruction on themes and/or genres, teachers offer a continuum of choices (for example, a less challenging, average, and more challenging work of historical fiction). Readability ranges within themes is the only way to make certain that every child consistently encounters books he or she is able to read. Less able readers exclusively listening to tape-recorded books or "buddy reading" chapters is not acceptable in our balanced model. A carefully selected range of choices allows teachers at each grade level to meet the indi-

Figure 2
Five-Finger Rule

If the child reads three paragraphs—one each from the beginning, middle, and end—from a prospective book and encounters five words per paragraph of which he or she is uncertain, the book may be too difficult at this time.

vidual needs of all readers—from gifted learners to children with specific learning disabilities.

At West Hanover, children will encounter mysteries, folklore, historical fiction, comedies, survival stories, contemporary fiction, biographies, nonfiction, and poetry repeatedly as they progress through the grades. For example, mysteries such as *Nate the Great* (Sharmat, 1972) are fun to solve in first grade, *Flatfoot Fox* (Clifford, 1990) and *Cam Jansen* (Adler, 1980) are the sleuths of choice in third grade, and by sixth grade *The Westing Game* challenges even the most reluctant pre-adolescent reader.

It is important to note that, with only a few exceptions, the genres that make up the literature collection vary little across grade levels. Efforts are taken to ensure that a balance of fiction, nonfiction, and poetry is available at each grade; nonfiction is important in first grade, and fiction is still enjoyed by sixth graders. Annual reviewing efforts by the teaching staff at West Hanover ensure that a balance of genres exists at each grade level.

Responding to Text

It became clear to us, through extensive professional reading and observing and through interaction with children that the acquisition of literacy is a language-driven, transactional process that can be enhanced by personally responding to text (Rosenblatt, 1994; Tierney & Mosenthal, 1983). As Rosenblatt states,

> Terms such as the reader are somewhat misleading, though convenient, fictions. There is no such thing as a generic reader or a generic literary work; there are in reality only the potential millions of individual readers of individual literary works.... The reading of any work of literature is, of necessity, an individual and unique occurrence involving the mind and emotions of some particular reader. (p. 1057)

Rosenblatt's model of reading and writing proposes that these processes are driven linguistically and call on the reader and/or writer to transact with text. She defines transaction as the nature of humans to interact continuously with their environment, mostly by using the capacity for language. Inherent in Rosenblatt's model are several key elements embraced at West Hanover:

1. Readers continuously transact with text, making choices and decisions, that result in the construction of meaning.

2. Writers also continuously transact with text, usually in a rule-governed fashion (using words, sentences, etc.) to construct meaning.

3. Though reading and writing overlap, they are also different cognitive processes.

4. Making "public" meaning of text, such as in an instructional setting, should be negotiated.

5. Instruction in both reading and writing should promote the view that they are holistic processes whose primary outcome is the construction of personal meaning.

Incorporating transactional theory into our framework meant that responding to text at every grade level would be personal, negotiated, and linguistically driven. Literature discussion groups, reading response logs, contracts, and response heuristics are just a few of the methods that encourage readers at West Hanover to transact with text.

Balance in Grades K-2

Words and Word Parts in Grades K-2

There were many instructional decisions made in connection with the primary program, but the one that caused the most concern and reflection was how to teach the letters and sounds of the alphabet. The early childhood literature (and an early childhood initiative elsewhere in the district) recommended incidental sound instruction and exposure to the alphabet as letters emerged within literature rather than in a prescribed order. We questioned the randomness of this approach and found solace in the research of linguists and cognitive psychologists who noted that language is predictable and rule-governed (Adams, 1990; Clay, 1985).

We reasoned that if children needed to use letters and sounds to read and write, our job was to make the orthography as sensible and predictable as possible. The question for us was not the sequence in which the alphabet was taught; we teach the letters and sounds of the alphabet in order. A much more important concern was the relationship between our instruction and the children's ability to use the alphabet in a meaningful way.

Since the reforms at West Hanover began, research continues to confirm the importance of spelling-sound patterns in the primary grades. Phonemic awareness among prereaders is a powerful predictor of future success in reading and spelling (Adams, 1990). Not only does it predict achievement in these areas better than IQ or perceptual development, but explicit exposure to phonemic awareness activities can improve reading achievement (Allington & Cunningham, 1998). In addition to sound analysis and blending, teaching concepts about print is crucial. Young children need to discuss print and how it is ordered and arranged. It is clear, however, that these opportunities for emerging readers have to be direct and meaningful and must occur only in the primary grades (Adams, 1990).

The purpose for providing direct instruction in the sounds and letters of the alphabet is to engage children in actual reading and writing. Letters and sounds are never presented in isolation. They are always taught in context, through literature, interactive writing, and journal writing. Similarities and differences between letters and sounds receive routine highlighting. Daily discussion occurs about how to use the alphabet to write. A number of the following letter characteristics are profiled frequently:

- consonants versus vowels
- placement of letters in the alphabet (beginning, middle, end; beside, between)

- spatial orientation of the letter (short, tall, etc.)
- associations (for example, the letter at the beginning of your name)

In addition to visual and/or auditory cueing, children are consistently encouraged to find letters and words in past journal entries, on word walls, and in books. Encountering letters and words in all types of print reminds young readers that written language is purposeful and meaningful.

At West Hanover, interactive writing (Clay, 1985) is paired with word walls of less decodable high-frequency words that emerging readers need. Interactive sentences are constructed together, passing the pen back and forth between teacher and students. The teacher guides the writing of words by referencing the word wall and helping students to "sound stretch" highly decodable words. Words such as *the*, *when*, and *where* remain on word walls throughout kindergarten. The first 10 to 15 words from Fry's Instant Words (Fry, Kress, & Fountoukidis, 1993) are placed on the word walls during the early months in kindergarten. More high-frequency words are added as needed or requested.

Systematic teaching of word recognition and vocabulary occurs at West Hanover. In first grade, the high-frequency words needed for early fluent reading are reviewed daily. Children often receive a "word play" book where weekly lists of words are pasted. The words are paired with a short poem. Daily review goes far beyond recognition and includes activities recommended by Weaver (1994) such as

- semantic cueing (find the opposite of…, find a word that means the same as…),
- phonemic cueing (which word has the same beginning sound as…),
- categorization (find all the words that mean the same as *big*), and
- interactive sentence writing (shared writing with sound stretching).

In second grade, this same high-frequency word instruction occurs as needed on an individual basis. Constructing word walls and interactive writing, however, occur consistently during the primary grades.

A wide variety of vocabulary techniques are used in our first and second grades. Semantic feature analysis (Pittelman, Heimlich, Berglund, & French, 1991), semantic mapping (Heimlich & Pittelman, 1986), text impression (Tierney, Readence, & Dishner, 1995), vocabulary anticipation (Marinak et al., 1998), and Other Words For (see Figure 3) are just a few of the activities used regularly to build and broaden vocabulary. The literature being read by the children determines the vocabulary-building activities chosen. For example, certain text lends itself to text impression while other books contain vocabulary well suited for semantic feature analysis. Successful vocabulary instruction does not seem to reside with one technique or another. Rather, balanced use of all these techniques—from teacher to teacher and grade level to grade level—seems to be the key to growing the vocabulary of emerging readers. (See Chapter 2 for further discussion on vocabulary instruction.)

Constructing Meaning in Grades K–2

Although words and word parts represent an extremely important component of the K–2 program, we never wanted to lose sight of read-

Figure 3
Other Words For...

This is an activity to broaden vocabulary as well as illustrate differences between more interesting and less interesting text. Consider constructing charts/walls that display "other words for" familiar nouns, verbs, and adjectives. Examples might include other words for *said*, *walk*, *happy*, etc. Invite children to add to the growing list by "reading for" or "listening for" additional words in the books you enjoy. Imagine how boring it would be if the only word an author used to describe conversation was *said*. Linguistic variety is what makes great literature compelling to read.

Figure 4
Reading Strategies and Methods in Grades K–2

Before Reading

Strategy	Method
Anticipate meaning	K-W-L
Create predictions	Text impression*
Anticipate vocabulary	Modified vocabulary sort*

During Reading

Strategy	Method
Confirm/adjust predictions	Revise/complete K-W-L
Construct meaning from fiction	Awareness of elements
Construct meaning from nonfiction	Awareness of elements
Use fix-up strategies	Guided reading*

After Reading

Strategy	Method
Retell	Story map
Summarize	Group summary
Evaluate	Group evaluation/review

ing as the ability to construct meaning from text. The wide variety of phonemic awareness and vocabulary activities we discovered or devised were necessary but far from sufficient for literacy learning.

Figure 4 presents the reading strategies used at each grade level at West Hanover and examples of instructional techniques we found most effective in grades K–2. These selected techniques are marked with an asterisk in the figure and are discussed in detail in this section.

Text impression (Tierney, Readence, & Dishner, 1995) is a thinking-reading technique that uses important or interesting vocabulary to guide prediction.

1. Before reading, the teacher selects a list of six to eight interesting words from an upcoming book.

2. The words are presented to the group, one by one, in the order they will appear in the book. As each word is presented, the teacher should guide students to form predictions about the text. Each carefully chosen word will help students hone their predictions.

3. Predictions are discussed by the group and recorded by the teacher. The teacher should note how predictions are modified and changed as each new word is added to the list.

4. The book is read by the teacher or students. The group then compares the author's use of the words with their predictions. The teacher should remind the children that some words can create many different ideas and that it is OK if their predictions do not match the text.

Modified vocabulary sort (Zuttell, 1998) is the deliberate act of formulating ideas about text-specific words that might be encountered in a reading selection.

1. Following a prereading discussion of an upcoming book, the teacher invites children to predict words that might be found in the text. The words are recorded on a chart by the teacher and then the book is read aloud.

2. After reading, the group compares predicted words with those found in the book.

3. The group should then decide on the words that must be known for a successful independent reading of the book, including high-frequency and text-specific words. The teacher should add important words the group might not offer.

4. Using the list, the teacher creates word cards for a vocabulary sort. Each child should receive a package of word cards containing the vocabulary from the list compiled together. The children then should sort the words on their desks by definition (a word that means), by word usage (the opposite or category), and by sound-symbol (all the words that begin with...).

Guided reading is a technique that revisits the format of a book or chapter and encourages re-reading and paraphrasing.

1. After students have read a book or chapter, the teacher conducts a guided reading discussion.
2. The discussion focuses on a series of six to eight questions (a blend of literal and inferential) that the teacher has created. These questions should move students from the beginning to the end of the book or chapter.
3. Teachers remind students to answer questions in their own words.
4. After answering questions in their own words, students are invited to re-read portions of the text that support their answer.

At West Hanover, our guided reading discussions are more explicit and teacher-directed than many of the guided reading practices in research literature (see, for example, Pinnell, 1985). During guided reading, we believe it is important to move children systematically through a book or chapter, to require answers in students' own words, and to support answers by having students orally read brief portions of text.

Flexible Grouping in Grades K-2

As part of our preparation for integrated language arts instruction, we visited many classrooms that were conducting some form of reading instruction that was alternative to basals. We observed primary classrooms that labeled themselves "whole language," "literature based," or "integrated language arts." Two patterns we discerned during our observations concerned us immediately—a lack of materials and a great deal of whole-class instruction. Clearly, it was important to have multiple copies of a wide variety of books. This provision was necessary to avoid whole-class reading instruction and to allow the use of flexible grouping. As Figure 5 illustrates, a number of important practices were incorporated into our primary model as a result of our observations.

Figure 5
Observations That Define West Hanover's Practices in Grades K-2

Kindergarten	
Observation	*Practice*
Kindergarten students are interested and excited by a variety of text.	Begin reading instruction in kindergarten.
The reading needs of 5-year-olds are as diverse as the reading needs in first and second grade.	Begin flexible grouping in kindergarten.
Kindergarten children are able to produce their own text.	Begin journal writing in kindergarten
Grades 1–2	
Observation	*Practice*
Primary grade students are interested and excited by a variety of text.	Offer a wide variety of books.
The reading needs and interests of primary grade children are highly diverse.	Group flexibly. Offer choice.
Primary grade children are able to produce a wide variety of text.	Continue journal writing. Introduce reading response logs.

Flexible grouping at West Hanover is defined as a balance of similar-ability grouping and mixed-ability grouping. However, the composition and duration of the flexible groups vary across the three primary grades.

In kindergarten, literature groups are driven by student choice. Children interact as a group based on the predictable language book they have chosen. In addition, small ability groups meet for phonemic awareness training.

In first grade, similar-ability and mixed-ability grouping may occur concurrently. On the same day, students may meet in a mixed-ability group for literature discussion and an ability group for phonemic activities. By the same token, students may be grouped (either mixed ability or similar ability) for the duration of a book or unit.

In late first grade and second grade (after children emerge as readers and when direct phonemic and word recognition review decreases), flexible grouping occurs based on need, interest, and choice. A *need group* is an ability group that is constructed by the teacher based on the instructional needs of the students. Children come together in a *choice group* because they have all chosen to read the same title. Finally, children are members of an *interest group* because they are all interested in a given topic (dinosaurs, rocks, etc.) and will work together to complete a project. A continuum of leveled literature is available to both the choice and interest groups. Generally, choice groups are constructed around works of fiction, and interest groups research a nonfiction topic. During the course of the entire school year, children spend approximately one third of their reading time in need groups, one third in choice groups, and one third in interest groups.

Text Selection in Grades K-2

Teaching with high-quality fiction and nonfiction is relatively straightforward. The only exception our teachers found was centered on the folklore genre. We found ourselves struggling with appropriate instructional categories for the wide array of tales that are shared. In order to categorize our fictional folklore appropriately, it was necessary to arrive at schoolwide definitions of the various types of folklore. A glossary was created using a number of sources, including *The Lincoln Writing Dictionary* (Morris, 1998) and *Children's Literature* (Huck, 1976). A few examples of glossary definitions follow:

Fairy tale: a short story that usually originated as an oral tale, and in which good and evil are clearly defined and good prevails. Fairy tales are usually recorded during the teller's lifetime.

Legend: a story about a seemingly real person, usually one who performs amazing or heroic feats.

Myth: a story originally told by early people to explain the features of the natural world.

Folk tale: a story that was told hundreds of years ago and passed down over time by word of mouth. Folk tales are the oldest form of literature. They began so far back in human history that it is often impossible to date them. Many folk tales tried to explain natural events (animal traits, floods) or human characteristics (greed, jealousy).

Having established a high-quality collection of children's literature at West Hanover, the staff began exploring ways to respond to the stories and informational text they were reading. Our goal focused on using consistent response strategies while offering enough variety and choice to keep students excited and motivated.

Responding to Text in Grades K-2

Responding to literature in the primary grades includes a balance of verbal and written responses. Verbal opportunities range from whole-class and small-group discussion in kindergarten and first grade to small-group and literature discussion groups in second grade.

Written responses in the primary grades include group-created stories, group fact books, individual response logs (two or three pages) and individual fact collections. The use of graphic organizers as a reading response begins in the primary grades. Primary teachers are careful, however, not to overuse graphic organizers. We found that an overreliance on preconstructed frames can result in abbreviated written responses. Teachers also attempt to focus student response by choosing interesting or unusual organizers. An example of one of our favorite

Figure 6
Character Map for *Where the Wild Things Are*

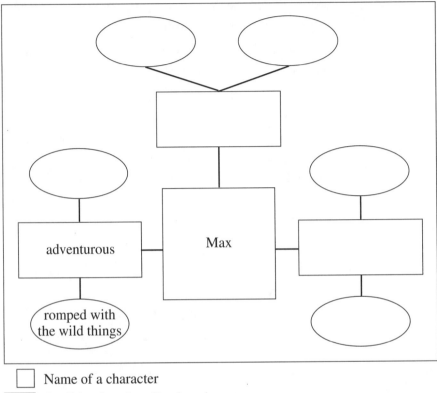

☐ Name of a character
▭ Qualities that describe that character
⬭ Examples of those qualities

primary organizers can be found in Figure 6. It is useful when a story contains one or more fascinating characters.

Balance in Grades 3-6

Words and Word Parts in Grades 3-6

In the intermediate grades at West Hanover, instruction in word-study strategies replaces the word recognition and phonemic awareness

---

activities taught in the primary grades. Included in word study are strategies to decode multisyllabic words, the use of context clues, and instruction in word origins.

We have found that even if teachers can convince children to copy definitions from the dictionary, such practice is not the most effective strategy for learning new meanings. Though the dictionary constitutes a necessary tool for vocabulary work, so too is the text in which the word occurs. Our alternative to copying new vocabulary words and their definitions is the word web in Figure 7. This graphic organizer requires readers to insert the new word and a word or phrase that will help them remember the new word. The word or phrase could be from the dictionary, another text, or preferably from the child's own prior

Figure 7
Word Web

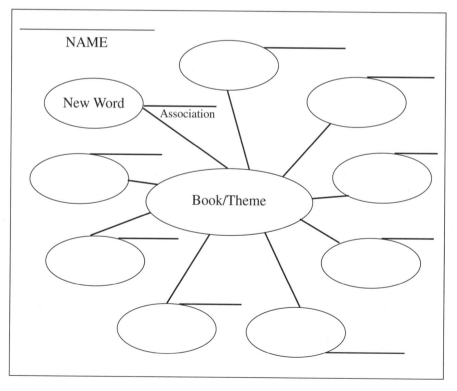

knowledge. These word webs, which will look different for every child, are fun to share as a group.

Vocabulary development is monitored carefully before, during, and after reading. Readers in the intermediate grades engage in a variety of vocabulary anticipation activities prior to reading. Once vocabulary has been introduced and discussed, teachers encourage and monitor the use of new words during guided reading discussion. Teachers model and expect the use of new vocabulary in written responses such as reading logs, summaries, and heuristics.

Constructing Meaning in Grades 3-6

Direct instruction and repeated modeling of reading strategies is the focus of literacy instruction in the intermediate grades at West Hanover. We believe that readers need frequent practice with each strategy in the framework. While providing many opportunities to use the strategies, it is also important for teachers to continually encourage strategic application to increasingly more difficult text. Intermediate grade readers, for example, should be expected to summarize a chapter in third and fourth grade, multiple chapters in fifth grade, and entire books by sixth grade.

Figure 8 presents the reading strategies used at each grade level and examples of instructional techniques we found most effective in grades 3–6. These selected techniques are marked with an asterisk in the figure and are discussed in detail in this section.

K-W-L Plus (Carr & Ogle, 1987) (What I know-What I want to know/what I learned) is a thinking-reading strategy that can be used with fiction or nonfiction (an example of a K-W-L strategy sheet is shown in Chapter 3, page 47). The "Plus" has been added to the original K-W-L to encourage the use of categorization and summarization.

1. Prior to completing a K-W-L Plus activity, teachers should set a purpose for reading and clearly explain what will be required after reading. The reading response required is important as students are asked to formulate questions and identify what still needs to be learned.

Figure 8
Reading Strategies and Methods in Grades 3-6

Before Reading

Strategy	*Method*
Anticipate meaning/create predictions	K-W-L Plus*
Anticipate vocabulary	Definitions templates

During Reading

Strategy	*Method*
Confirm/adjust predictions	Revise/complete K-W-L Plus*
Construct meaning from fiction	Awareness of elements
Construct meaning from nonfiction	Awareness of text structures*
Use fix-up strategies	Guided reading*
	Fix-up continuum*

After Reading

Strategy	*Method*
Retell	Story pyramid
Summarize/evaluate	Response heuristic*

2. Before reading, teachers should ask students to consider what they know about a book, subject, or topic. Teachers should record student responses in the *What I know* column.

3. Following this brainstorming, teachers should continue the before reading discussion by asking students what they want to find out. Once again, this information is recorded by teachers in the *What I want to know* column.

4. After completing the first two columns of the K-W-L Plus, teachers should model categorizing the information offered by students.

5. After reading, teachers ask students what was learned or still needs to be learned about the topic or subject, and complete

the third column of the sheet. This is an excellent time for teachers to help students identify additional resources that might be needed for future research or reading.

Awareness of text structures (Marinak, Moore, Henk, & Keepers, 1998) enhances the ability to construct meaning from nonfiction (literature and/or textbooks).

1. Teachers should provide instruction in, and practice using, the five elements of nonfiction and the four text structures around which the elements are organized. The elements of nonfiction include author's purpose, major ideas, supporting details, important vocabulary, and the use of reader's aids. The text structures of nonfiction are enumeration, time order, compare/contrast, and cause/effect.

2. Teachers should include the use of a wide variety of graphic organizers during instruction in the elements and text structures.

3. When having students practice the identification of text structures, teachers should provide them with short pieces of text that contain readily discernible structure. Children's literature and children's magazines typically are excellent resources for well-organized nonfiction material.

Guided reading in the intermediate grades becomes a framework for literature discussion. This technique evolved as a way of guiding reading without requiring students to write the answers to comprehension questions. Our intermediate grade guided reading facilitates purposeful reading, paraphrasing, and re-reading.

1. Prior to reading, students should be provided with four to six questions about the chapter or passage. The instructor can provide the questions or a Q-Matrix (Kagan, 1990) can be completed by the students to formulate their own questions. The Q-Matrix is a cooperative learning activity that provides participants with the stems necessary to formulate higher-order questions. The question stems are generic and can be applied to any type of text.

Marinak and Henk

2. Students then should read silently the assigned pages or chapter. Their responsibility is to come to discussion group having read the chapter or passage, formulated an answer to each question in their head, and recorded information on the organizer shown in Figure 9. The organizer requires students to write the page number, paragraph number, and the first three words where the re-reading will begin.

Figure 9
Guided Reading

Name _____

Book title _____

Date _____

- -

1. Question

_____

_____

_____

_____

Answer

   Page Number _____

   Paragraph Number _____

   First Three Words _____

2. Question

_____

_____

_____

_____

Answer

   Page Number _____

   Paragraph Number _____

   First Three Words _____

3. During the group discussion, students share and talk about their answers. They are encouraged by the teacher to answer the questions in their own words. To support their answer, students re-read portions of the text.

Fix-up continuum (Davey & Porter, 1982) encourages readers to self-assess their ability to use fix-up strategies when attempting to regain meaning. These strategies include re-reading, adjusting rate, and asking for help.

Fix-Up Continuum
1 = I do understand and could explain what I have read to others.
2 = I sort of understand but probably could not explain what I have read to others.
3 = I don't understand.

Following are options for students when their self-assessment is a 2 or 3.
• re-read (orally/silently)
• partner read with a friend
• discuss material with a friend
• ask teacher for help

1. Teachers should repeatedly model the fix-up continuum using think-alouds with a variety of text.

2. Following teacher modeling, students are encouraged to self-assess their comprehension using the continuum. This self-evaluation can be done orally during discussion groups or in reading response logs.

Response heuristic (Tierney, Readence, & Dishner, 1995) allows the reader to summarize major ideas in an abbreviated form, integrate them with prior knowledge, and personally react to them. The strategy was a welcome addition to our intermediate grade instruction. With several books being read, the heuristic provided our teachers with a response framework that could be tailored to any text at any grade level.

The response heuristic asks students to react in writing to a three-part format: (1) text perceptions, (2) reactions to the text, and (3) associations with the text.

Text perceptions tend to be summary statements about important information from the text (for example, *Mr. Cory was a man admired by all*).

Reactions to the text are evaluative statements that ask students to express how they feel about text or story information (for example, *I agree that Mr. Cory's actions were admirable*).

Association with text are higher level evaluations that require students to associate information with their own prior knowledge or associate the current reading with past readings (for example, *Mr. Cory reminds me of *character* in *story**).

1. Teachers should repeatedly model the response heuristic with a book being read aloud to the class.

2. Following a period of modeling, teachers should encourage students to use the heuristic on a daily basis as a framework for their reading response log entries. The response expectations can range from single sentences in third grade, to paragraphs and multiple paragraphs in the upper-intermediate grades.

3. As an ongoing model for students, teachers might consider keeping a teacher log constructed using the response heuristic. The log could be kept on a book being read by the class.

Flexible Grouping in Grades 3-6

In preparation for moving away from the basal and from ability grouping, intermediate grade teachers also read relevant research, participated in professional discussion groups, and completed observations in classrooms across the area. Figure 10 on the next page presents a summary of the observations and discussion points that define West Hanover's current grouping practices.

As a result of the continuum of literature present in every theme/genre unit, flexible grouping in the intermediate grades is driven

---

Figure 10
Observations That Define West Hanover's Practices in Grades 3-6

Grades 3–6	
Observation	*Practice*
Book choice is paramount for intermediate grade readers.	Allow as much choice as possible.
One title being read by the entire class cannot meet individual needs.	Build a range of literature that meets the readability needs of all readers.
Content can overwhelmingly drive literature offerings.	Avoid relying on a content area to drive book selections (e.g., too much historical fiction when U.S. history is taught).
Struggling readers are not necessarily struggling writers in the intermediate grades.	Balance responding options to include writing, discussion, and performance.

more by student choice than by teacher choice. Mixed-ability groups will change with each new theme/genre. Groups are constructed based on the title(s) selected by students. To meet the needs of every student, teachers provide two or three student-choice groups within each theme/genre. Daily reading/writing conferences represent yet another grouping option teachers use to address individual literacy needs.

Text Selection in Grades 3-6

Again, with only a few exceptions, the genres that comprise the literature collection vary little across intermediate grade levels. Efforts are ongoing to ensure that a balance of fiction (contemporary, fantasy, comedy, historical, etc.), nonfiction, and poetry is available at each grade level. It became clear to our intermediate grade teachers, however, that the teaching of fiction and nonfiction must include far more than the standard elements.

To comprehend a variety of fiction in the intermediate grades, readers need to understand subtle differences that occur across the story elements (that is, characters, setting, problem, events, resolution). As a result, when we teach fiction genres, our teachers provide readers with a framework for the type of fiction being read. Comparing and contrasting the types of fiction across the elements can then occur. For example, the elements are not weighted equally in importance across the various genres of fiction. Figure 11 contains two of our instructional frameworks that illustrate this point.

To assist our readers in constructing meaning from nonfiction literature as well as from their science and social studies books, our

Figure 11
Comparison of Two Instructional Frameworks

Fantasy	Historical Fiction
Characters Fanciful; may be supernatural.	*Characters* Realistic; believable for period.
Setting Real or imagined; past, present, future.	*Setting* Realistic; taking place in past.
Problem Subtly presented; may be unbelievable.	*Problem* Directly presented; believable for period.
Events Actions may shift rapidly; may be surreal.	*Events* Driven by human actions/ events.
Resolution May not be resolved.	*Resolution* Problem is resolved. Resolution is historically sound.

teaching had to be far more inclusive than a mere reminder of the elements of nonfiction (author's purpose, major ideas, supporting details, use of reader's aids, and important vocabulary). In addition, direct instruction in the four text structures of nonfiction (enumeration, time order, compare/contrast, and cause/effect) is taught repeatedly across the intermediate grades. By repeating text structure instruction at all intermediate grades with a variety of titles, teachers can make nonfiction as predictable as fiction. Readers learn that certain topics lend themselves more to some structures than others. For example, one can expect to encounter material during an endangered animals unit that is organized around the text structures of enumeration and compare/contrast. A weather unit, on the other hand, can be organized almost exclusively using a cause/effect structure.

A number of graphic organizers have been designed throughout the years to help our intermediate grade readers access and use the text structures of nonfiction. Figure 12 is an example of a compare/contrast organizer. This particular frame reminds teachers and students that the concept of "attribute" is crucial when comparing and contrasting.

Responding to Text in Grades 3-6

Responding to literature in the intermediate grades includes many opportunities to write, discuss, and perform. Literature discussion groups occur regularly at all grade levels at West Hanover. Reading response logs and the use of response heuristics are the most common types of written responses. We learned, however, that reading response logs can be just as tedious and uninteresting as workbook pages. As it became clear that we were unintentionally eroding any enthusiasm our intermediate grade readers may have had for literature responding, we constructed five "commandments" for the use of reading response logs.

1. Arrange for each book or story to have a separate reading response. Long composition books and three-ring binders of endless responses destroy motivation. Just as in the primary grades, intermediate grade readers need to feel completion. The fin-

Figure 12
Compare/Contrast Organizer

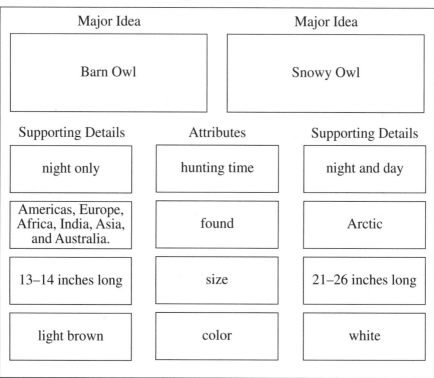

ished log should be shared with the child's family, peers, and principal, and then placed in a portfolio.

2. Vary response options during a log. This variety includes responding with paragraphs, illustrations, maps, and lists, within one log. In addition, there is the need to balance guided responses (teacher questions) with personal responses.

3. Use an array of questioning strategies. Offer teacher-made questions along with the option for student-generated questions (Q-Matrix).

4. Vary logs across books. Try to match the style of the log with the book(s) being read. For example, a dialogue journal works

well when two characters are conversing, as in *I'll Meet You At the Cucumbers* (Moore, 1992). A letter or diary log, on the other hand, might be perfect when one character is struggling alone as in *The True Confessions of Charlotte Doyle* (Avi, 1992). Log options might include, but are not limited to the following:

- diaries/journals (first-person reflections)
- dye-cut books (cut to establish a pattern or sequence)
- chapter logs (a log completed for important chapters)
- envelope books (a series of letters and envelopes bound as a log)
- atlases (a series of maps illustrating changing settings)
- dictionaries (a dictionary of important or interesting words)
- interviews (between characters or classmates)
- buddy logs (with responses from peers and/or teacher)

5. Maintain accountability for grade-level spelling, punctuation, and capitalization. Accountability in spelling should include high-frequency words and text-specific vocabulary that can be referenced easily.

The Story Continues

The journey of West Hanover Elementary School toward balanced literacy instruction certainly ranks as a meaningful and intriguing one. Beginning with a traditional basal reader program, the teachers opened their minds and hearts to an altogether different philosophy of language learning. Along the way they immersed themselves in the professional literature on innovative literacy practices and seized every opportunity to learn as much as possible about these new ways of plying their craft. Not satisfied with merely reading about teachers and schools on the cutting edge, these teachers visited classrooms where they hoped to witness whole language in action. In addition, they attended seminars, workshops, inservices, and conferences, and enrolled in graduate courses in literacy. Without question, they set their sights on creating and implementing a fully articulated whole language program. From reading and hearing about the travels of other teachers who were inclined similarly, they knew that becoming whole language teachers would take years to achieve. And although the prospect of the long voyage was surely daunting, they nonetheless committed to the challenge.

To their credit, the West Hanover teachers realized that it would be necessary to make the transition to whole language gradually. Their plan involved deliberately easing first to a middle ground, in accordance with the growth of their literacy-related knowledge and pedagogical skills. Even so, they became swept up in the excitement of profound and pervasive change, and their passion for the new philosophy ran high. Fortunately, though, they exercised maturity in tempering their zeal against the backdrop of personal insecurities and a professional resolve to "get it right."

Over time, trial and error drove the change process at West Hanover. Although the teachers benefited from accounts of whole language researchers, much of what they attempted instructionally represented new ground for them. Whole language in the United States had struggled in its infancy, and as a result, best practices remained a veritable mystery even for the most experienced and accomplished literacy professionals. The teachers at West Hanover were no exception. As a result, their efforts, however well intentioned, met with a fair share of both success and failure. Effective methods emerged and warranted retention. By the same token, unsuccessful methods and interventions revealed themselves, fell into disfavor, and rightly gave way to alternative means of promoting literacy growth in the children.

The West Hanover teachers, in refining their day-to-day practice, arrived at what might be called "balanced literacy" more by hard work and ongoing reflection than by design. The methods and procedures that worked for these teachers came to be virtual destinations in their own right. The teachers simply made a good faith attempt to test prevailing theory and apply it in practice, paying careful attention to the impact their overarching approach exerted on children's literacy acquisition. They settled on what intuitively felt right to them. When in doubt, the children's thoughts, deeds, and actions provided guidance.

The teachers had prepared for one fascinating destination only to find that a more proximal, yet exotic port-of-call best suited their needs.

Although the methods described in this chapter have worked extremely well for West Hanover Elementary School, they may not necessarily function as well in other educational contexts. For this reason, readers must resist the temptation to treat this account of a successful literacy transition as a prescriptive template for implementation elsewhere. No two school cultures are identical. Schools can vary by a myriad of factors that could radically alter the kind of literacy instruction that should be provided. Social, historical, economic, psychological, philosophical, demographic, and political factors all set the stage for different literacy outcomes.

It also is important to recognize that what works well now at West Hanover may not suffice in the school's near or long-term future. There is no telling how the program will need to evolve over time. The only certainty is that the teaching staff must continue to place the needs of the children first and make whatever adjustments necessary to help them achieve their full literacy potential.

The teachers know that their personal journeys must continue. They believe that becoming balanced literacy teachers requires the same long, probably endless process of enlightenment and maturation associated with whole language teaching. Regardless of where teachers fall philosophically along a literacy approach continuum, complacency must give way to vision, sensitivity, and follow through. Proactivity must prevail.

It is important to note that the West Hanover story represents only one version of what might be termed balanced literacy. Clearly there is no definitive consensus in the field about this evasive concept. It seems that in some circles balance hinges on the degree to which phonics instruction is separate or contextualized or whether meaning construction is a precursor to decoding or vice versa (Freppon & Dahl, 1998). In fact, judgments about balance depend on a host of instructional variables (Bottomley, Truscott, Marinak, Henk, & Melnick, 1998; Thelan, 1995). For instance, the question of who selects the materials must be considered. It would seem that although teachers select much of what students read and write about in balanced classrooms, students do have self-selection opportunities. Authenticity of tasks impacts balance as well. Students do engage in authentic tasks and respond in a variety of formats; however, worksheets selected or designed by the teacher may still play a role. Moreover, in balanced approaches, direct instruction of various types is invoked as needed—although not according to a scope and sequence chart or necessarily within a meaningful context. Like whole language, writing takes on a process focus in these classrooms and grouping remains flexible. Thematic instruction does occur in balanced literacy contexts, but the themes tend to be more narrow and center around distinct topics and single books. And, in terms of assessment, teachers find a middle ground between authentic forms of evaluation and more traditional measures such as tests.

The West Hanover version of balanced literacy can be characterized as not just a single balance between phonics and whole language or between skills and strategies. Balanced reading instruction in the school is a framework of effective literacy instruction that contains many balances. Attempts are made to balance grouping patterns (whole class, small group, one-on-one) and types of text (fiction, nonfiction, poetry). A balance of teacher-choice and student-choice can be seen in the selection of literature and reading responses. And lastly, the assessment that informs our instruction is a combination of student self-evaluation, portfolio collections, and standardized measures.

Clearly the evolution of West Hanover Elementary School as a successful balanced literacy program is a tribute to its teachers. These dedicated professionals kept their children's welfare squarely in mind. Intuitions and preferences gave way to tangible and objective assessments of children's academic performance and attitudes toward literacy. If the journey of this one school is at all instructive, the lesson rests on the critical importance of teachers who care about children and take pride in their practice. In this sense, the teachers exhibited a willingness not only to break new ground, but also to persevere in the face of formidable political and social pressures. Without question, they made a firm and unwavering commitment to enhancing the quality of children's literacy. And that has made all the difference.

Author Note

The transformation of West Hanover Elementary School from traditional reading practices to more balanced literacy instruction would not have been possible without the knowledge and support of the building administrator, Mr. John R. Baumgardner. We are grateful for his vision.

REFERENCES

Adams, M.J. (1990). *Beginning to read: Thinking and learning about print.* Cambridge, MA: Massachusetts Institute of Technology Press.

Allington, R. (1983). The reading instruction provided readers of differing abilities. *The Elementary School Journal, 83,* 556–561.

Allington, R., & Cunningham, P. (1998). *Classrooms that work.* Portsmouth, NH: Heinemann.

Bottomley, D.M., Truscott, D.M., Marinak, B.A., Henk, W.A., & Melnick, S.A. (1998). An affective comparison of whole language, literature-based, and basal literacy instruction. *Reading Research and Instruction, 38*(2), 115–129..

Carr, E., & Ogle, D. (1987). K-W-L Plus: A strategy for comprehension and summarization. *Journal of Reading, 30,* 626–631.

Clay, M. (1985). *The early detection of reading difficulties.* Auckland, New Zealand: Heinemann.

Davey, B., & Porter, S.M. (1982). Comprehension-rating: A procedure to assist poor comprehenders. *Journal of Reading, 26,* 197–202.

Deci, E.L., Vallerand, R., Pelletier, L., & Ryan, R. (1991). Motivation and education: The self-determination perspective. *Educational Psychologist, 26,* 325–347.

Freppon, P., & Dahl, K. (1998). Balanced instruction: Insights and considerations. *Reading Research Quarterly, 33,* 240–251.

Fry, E., Kress, J., & Fountoukidis, D. (1993). *The reading teacher's book of lists.* New York: Simon & Schuster.

Heimlich, J.E., & Pittelman, S.D. (1986). *Semantic mapping: Classroom applications.* Newark, DE: International Reading Association.

Hiebert, E.H. (1983). An examination of ability grouping for reading instruction. *Reading Research Quarterly, 18,* 231–255.

Huck, C. (1976). *Children's literature.* New York: Holt, Rinehart and Winston.

Kagan, S. (1990). *Cooperative learning.* San Juan Capistrano, CA: Resources for Teachers.

Lipson, M., & Wixson, K. (1997). *Assessment and instruction of reading and writing disability.* New York: Longman.

Marinak, B.A., Moore, J.C., & Henk, W.A., & Keepers, M. (1998). *The Pennsylvania System of State Assessment: Reading instructional handbook.* Harrisburg, PA: Pennsylvania Department of Education.

Ogle, D.M. (1986). K-W-L: A teaching model that develops active reading of informational text. *The Reading Teacher, 39,* 564–570.

Pinnell, G.S. (1985). Helping teachers help children at risk: Insights from the Reading Recovery program. *Peabody Journal of Education, 62,* 70–85.

Pittelman, S.D., Heimlich, J.E., Berglund, R.L., & French, M.P. (1991). *Semantic feature analysis: Classroom applications.* Newark, DE: International Reading Association.

Rosenblatt, L.M. (1983). *Literature as exploration.* New York: Modern Language Association.

Rosenblatt, L. (1994). The transactional theory of reading and writing. In R.B. Ruddell, M.R. Ruddell, H. Singer (Eds.), *Theoretical models and processes of reading* (4th ed., pp. 1057–1092). Newark, DE: International Reading Association.

Slavin, R.E. (1983). *Cooperative learning.* New York: Longman.

Tierney, R., & Mosenthal, J. (1983). The cohesion concept's relationship to coherence of text. *Research in the Teaching of English, 17*(3), 215–229.

Tierney, R., Readence, J., & Dishner, E. (1995). *Reading strategies and practices.* Boston, MA: Allyn & Bacon.

Weaver, C. (1994). *Reading process and practice.* Portsmouth, NH: Heinemann.

CHILDREN'S LITERATURE REFERENCES

Adler, D. (1980). *Cam Jansen.* New York: Penguin.

Avi. (1992). *The true confessions of Charlotte Doyle.* New York: Avon.

Clifford, E. (1990). *Flatfoot fox.* New York: Random House.

Moore, L. (1992). *I'll meet you at the cucumbers.* New York: Bantam Doubleday.

Morris, C. (1998). *The Lincoln writing dictionary.* New York: Harcourt Brace.

Raskin, E. (1978). *The westing game.* New York: Penguin.

Sendak, M. (1963). *Where the wild things are.* New York: HarperCollins.

Sharmat, M. (1972). *Nate the great.* New York: Bantam Doubleday.

CHAPTER 9

The Balancing Act: Balanced Reading Instruction In Action

Kathryn A. Williams

Now that you have read the different perspectives on balanced reading programs offered in this book, how can you initiate a balanced program in your school? The starting point is you and your classroom. A clear sense of purpose and what you need to accomplish is critical. This final chapter reviews the philosophy, major elements, and models of balanced reading instruction that provide evidence that all children can be successful in literacy acquisition.

Professional interest in promoting balanced reading instruction has spread throughout the world over the past several years. Abundant research, international in scope and interdisciplinary in nature, has led many educators to view a balanced approach as the most sensible and effective approach to reading instruction (Adams, 1990; Au, Carroll, & Scheu, 1998; Clay, 1993; Freppon & Dahl, 1998; Heilman, Blair, & Rupley, 1998).

Although this view of balanced instruction now seems to have wide acceptance, this has not always been the case. For many years, continuing debate in literacy circles centered on what is the most appropriate way to teach children reading acquisition. The debate was especially vigorous between proponents of code-emphasis approaches and proponents of meaning emphasis approaches. Within the debate, the two separate issues of how children learn to read and how children should be taught to read often became intertwined and indistinguishable (Iversen, 1994). Fortunately researchers in reading acquisition, cognitive processing, motivation theory, learning strategies, and other forms of literacy acquisition (writing, spelling, speech) have given us overwhelming evidence to support the case for balancing reading instruction.

Many educators have not only endorsed the concept for balance, but they also are working to carry out balanced programs of reading instruction in their classrooms and schools. The questions asked most commonly during this implementation are "*What* is balanced in a balanced reading program? *How* does balanced reading instruction look in actual practice? and How do I go about carrying out a balanced reading program in my classroom?" This volume was compiled for the purpose of helping professional educators answer these questions.

Principles of Balanced Reading Instruction

The principles of "balance" are not nearly as simplistic as some might first envision. A truly balanced approach to literacy instruction does not mean merely including a phonics component with a literature emphasis program or adding some reading from "real" books to a basal program (Williams, 1998). It does call for teachers who are knowledgeable about language acquisition, literacy processes, instructional approaches, materials, metacognitive strategies, motivational techniques, curriculum design, assessment, and developmentally appropriate practice.

The chapters of this text reveal the balanced reading concept to be a dynamic model based on phonological processing of information needed to unlock the code, exposure to print, and problem-solving (metacognitive) strategies. Iversen (1996) describes the three major components as "intersecting and overlapping" and dynamic because they are not discrete or fixed and offer the user choice.

Along with the recognition and incorporation of the knowledge that the learner brings to the reading task and the knowledge that the teacher wishes to impart, the balanced reading model includes a very conscious attempt to teach children metacognitive knowledge (Iversen, 1996, 1997; Iversen & Reeder, 1998). This is the component that is traditionally missing from many classrooms. Iversen (1996) cites the following example of how a child might use the three essential types of metacognitive knowledge (declarative, procedural, and conditional or contextual) and how this then becomes the basis for the teacher to plan further instruction for the child.

> A child in the early stages of learning to write wishes to write the word *cake* in his/her story. This child has certain options open that will employ different strategies. At the declarative level the child may know that s/he can sound the word out and write what s/he hears. The child may also know that if s/he can say a known word that rhymes with *cake*, that word will probably be spelled the same way.
>
> The child then needs to use procedural knowledge to spell the word using the chosen method. If the child chooses to sound the word and write what is known, s/he has to know how to segment the word into its constituent phonemes (sounds) and write the graphemes (letters) that correspond to the given phonemes. If the child chooses to use a rhyming analogy, s/he has to know how to write the known word, how to segment the onset, that is, the initial letter/letter cluster, from the rime or rhyming segment of the word, how to substitute another initial letter or cluster, and how to combine the new onset with the existing rime to make a new word.
>
> To use conditional knowledge, the child has to know which of these strategies is the most appropriate to use in the situation. Again the child has several options. If the child does not know how to spell any words that rhyme with *cake*, although s/he knows that the procedure is available, that option is not available. If s/he uses that sounding out strategy, it may lead to a spelling of *kak* or *cak*, whereas rime analogy from *make* will probably result in the correct spelling. The rime analogy option however would not hold true for words with the same sound but different spelling patterns such as *care*, *bear*, *hair*. (pp. 13–14.)

This example shows clearly that the teacher must engage the child in conversation that reveals the child's thinking. The teacher then can design and use appropriate instruction that will help the child grow in strategic ability.

What Kind of Balance?

When thinking about balanced reading instruction you may first picture a balance scale. Yet you must consider that balanced reading instruction does not mean giving equal weight or equal time to phonics and whole language. It does call for teachers to be reflective and selective and use their knowledge of appropriate practice in helping all of their students to acquire literacy (Cheek, Flippo, & Lindsey, 1997). The balance described in this book by those practicing balanced reading instruction can more accurately be envisioned as the balance that must be achieved by a conductor of an orchestra when conducting a symphony. Not only must the conductor be knowledgeable in regard to what must be achieved, he or she must transmit this knowledge to the orchestra. The conductor also must consider the ability of each musician and what instruction or directions each musician needs in order to achieve the desired results. Indeed many elements must be considered and balanced. In a balanced reading program, some students will need more direct, intense phonics instruction, while others will already have or will easily acquire the necessary phonological awareness when they arrive in the classroom. Likewise, reading ability and reading acquisition rates vary from student to student. The teacher in a balanced reading program makes provision not only for the type, but also for the amount of instruction that must be done through orchestrating or balancing the amount of reading that is done to, with, and by each student (Reutzel & Cooter, 1999).

Balanced reading instruction is not simply a blending of approaches or an eclectic view. It is based on knowledge and reflection teamed with decision making and appropriate practice. Balanced reading instruction as described in this text is based on solid research and practice and has resulted in high rates of literacy in New Zealand and other countries (Anderson, Hiebert, Scott, & Wilkinson, 1985). The chapters of this text illustrate how balanced reading instruction can and does work in a variety of settings.

Many educators who theoretically endorse a balanced approach to reading instruction find that carrying out a truly balanced instructional program calls for much thought and careful planning. Classroom teachers responsible for planning the day-to-day reading program as well as those responsible for teacher education programs and courses have independently set forth to establish literacy programs that are striving for the "balance" described in theory. Experiences of some of these teachers have been presented in this volume to help others as they too attempt to achieve balanced reading instruction in their classroom.

As Dixie Lee Spiegel emphasizes in Chapter 1, there is no exact formula for reading instruction. However, the task does not have to be a continual guessing game or one of trial and error. Balanced approaches allow us to stop searching for that one program that works for all children all the time. Balanced approaches help us meet the needs of most children because they involve more than choosing between whole language and explicit strategy and skill instruction (Spiegel, 1998). We are now aware of a number of other critical aspects of balanced reading instruction, such as balance between learner-centered discovery and teacher-directed instruction; between planned and unplanned instruction; between small-group and whole-group interactions; between student-selected and teacher-selected materials; and between authentic assessment and standardized, norm-referenced assessment (Spiegel, 1994). Because effective balanced approaches are based on research—all research, not just one viewpoint or the latest "hot" topics (Cassidy & Wenrich, 1998)—they are by nature dynamic and responsive to new issues without abandoning what research has shown to be most effective.

Balanced approaches to literacy development are decision-making models in which an informed and thoughtful teacher makes choices every day about the best way to help each student advance as a reader and writer. This is why no two of the highly successful balanced programs described in this text are identical. Although those who developed the programs may have had similar philosophies and intentions, the balance had to be tailored to their own set of circumstances and the needs of their students. Effective balanced reading programs are flexible and responsive to the needs of students and to the components of a particular program. This means that the teacher is key to the success of a balanced program. Balanced literacy approaches are based on the view that the teacher is an informed decision maker, willing to take risks and responsibility. This teacher must be flexible and willing to grow and change when necessary. A teacher in a balanced reading program must be knowledgeable of various ways to critically and fairly evaluate students and to follow through with appropriate action based on identified needs. This process is not always easy, but it is effective.

Educational research and scientific technology have shown us a great deal more about how children learn and develop than ever before. We also have made great strides in knowing how literacy is acquired (Barr, Kamil, Mosenthal, & Pearson, 1991; Gough, Ehri, & Treiman, 1992; Williams, 1993). Research has given us insight into motivation techniques, learning environments, and other aspects of schools and schooling (Allington & Cunningham, 1996; Baker, Afflerbach, & Reinking, 1996). A balanced approach to literacy considers all these elements and pulls together this knowledge to form a comprehensive and flexible program supported by research (Spiegel, 1998). The chapters of this text provide evidence that the planning and work necessary to establish a balanced reading program is well worth the effort. The satisfaction of seeing the children in your classroom become successful readers and writers is hard to match.

We must recognize there is, for some, a down side to implementing a balanced reading instruction program. It is not a "quick fix" or "silver bullet" solution (Allington & Walmsley, 1995; Spiegel, 1998). Hopefully you already have determined that learning to read and write is too complex and too individual for there to be one universal activity or approach that will ensure that all children can learn to read and write well. A balanced approach recognizes that many factors influence literacy acquisition and accepts the contributions of many different approaches and perspectives. It ensures that effective procedures and practices are not discarded simply because a newer, more promising method has become popular. However, it does necessitate that the answer to the question "How do I begin?" be an individual one. Each teacher must analyze fairly their current literacy program, curriculum structure, classroom policies, and personal practices in light of the criteria for "balance." Once it is determined what changes are necessary to create an effective balanced reading program within their own classroom, creating the changes that will give this effective balance may take time and considerable effort.

This text has been written not only to inform and encourage implementation of more balanced reading programs but also to help you counteract these possible inhibitors to your implementation of a balanced program in your classroom or school. The authors have presented balanced programs that have provided consistent success often beyond what the authors first envisioned. Each of these programs is based on research. Each program took vision, planning, and work to implement. Each program recognizes that teachers are the key to successful literacy instruction; they must be informed decision makers who can be flexible in their teaching and assessing of students. Each program views literacy acquisition as comprehensive.

This comprehensive view of literacy is based on several important principles that in summary tell us that reading and writing are interrelated and interactive language processes and that literacy instruction should capitalize on this relationship (International Reading Association & National Council of Teachers of English, 1996). Instruction also should "lead children to understand that reading is a meaningful, active, and strategic process" (Heilman, Blair, & Rupley, 1998).

Although the programs described in this text are somewhat different, the underlying philosophies and intentions are very similar. They were designed around the recognition that there is great diversity among students, that appropriate instruction to accommodate the wide range of individual differences in the classroom is possible, and that given a well-balanced instructional climate and appropriate instruction all students can be successful in learning to read (Cheek, Flippo, & Lindsey 1997; Cunningham, Moore, Cunningham, & Moore, 1995; Heilman, Blair, & Rupley, 1998; Pressley, Rankin, & Yokoi, 1996).

A main characteristic of a balanced literacy program is that it teaches students what they need to know through the use of a variety of strategies, materials, and teaching approaches. There is also recognition that to a large extent, literacy acquisition is a developmental process in which children move through various sequential (although somewhat overlapping), predictable stages of reading development (Chall, 1996). However, some literacy skills may be learned within a wide span of time. Thus, balanced reading programs teach children developmentally relevant literacy skills within the context of appropriately leveled reading materials that are of interest to the students. Because of the flexibility within the balanced reading program model, there is room for a variety of interpretations. In planning appropriate instruction, teachers may draw from their own teaching strengths and preferences while paying attention to which reading skills are prerequisite and sequential, and which are more flexible in terms of instructional timing and the developmental stages of their students (Reutzel & Cooter, 1999).

Within a balanced instructional framework there will be meaningful skill instruction dealing with reading and study strategies, vocabulary and language, comprehension and decoding—all based on the needs within the classroom—not on getting through the book or a particular program or set of lessons. To gain insight into your students it is critical for you to have a plan for continuous assessment. Chapter 5 of this volume offers many ideas for obtaining information to inform instruction. Even those of you who already have a workable assessment plan may find ideas in Chapter 5 useful to incorporate and balance what you already do.

Teacher as Decision Maker

It is vital that classroom teachers, those in charge of teacher preparation programs, and those responsible for promoting reading instruction programs and practices understand that a balanced program is a complex blending of elements that include the actual learning environment, guidance practices, assessment, motivation, curriculum, beliefs about language and literacy acquisition, and more. A balanced program is not simplistic, undisciplined, eclectic thinking, but with planning, organization, and knowledge it can be implemented effectively. Putting all the teaching strategies together is not as difficult as it may seem. Think in terms of the four-step teaching cycle (see Figure 1). Keeping this continuous cycle in mind allows you to help children to rapidly gain reading and writing independence.

A balanced approach does provide freedom to use the most appropriate and effective approaches and methodologies to teach literacy, but it also requires breadth and depth of knowledge and willingness to take responsibility through choice. This can be frightening and confusing. A teacher must be willing to evaluate honestly and fairly and choose instruction responsibly. Should student-centered discovery methods or teacher-directed instruction be used? Does the learner need to concentrate on word elements or whole text? Will whole-group instruction be best or is this a time when small-group instruction would be most effective? Should I teach a particular strategy to this child or should I just teach him or her the word? Should the child be allowed to decide on the story, book, or activity he or she will read or do next or

Figure 1
The Teaching Cycle

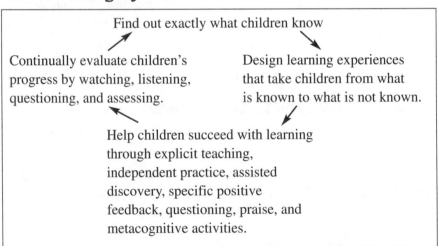

Adapted from Iversen, S., & Reeder, T. (1998). *Organizing for a literacy hour: Quality learning and teaching time.* Bothell, WA: The Wright Group.

would it be more appropriate for me to present material and instruction based on his or her choice? These are the kinds of questions decision-making teachers must be willing to ask. They must then be willing to search for appropriate answers based on research and their own knowledge of the learner and appropriate practices and take responsibility for making informed choices in regard to instruction.

It is clear that the programs described in this text are based on a concept of balance that is based on this more complex blending of factors related to reading success. These factors include modeling and reading aloud to students; language experience; shared, guided, and independent reading; as well as interactive, response and independent writing. These elements must be used and blended appropriately into a well-designed and structured balanced reading program.

This text was written to help you understand the balanced perspective of reading instruction and to help you evaluate your own literacy program in regard to this balance. We invite you to use the experiences described in this book to help you plan and carry out your instructional program that offers maximum success for all your students.

REFERENCES

Adams, M.J. (1990). *Beginning to read: Thinking and learning about print.* Cambridge, MA: Massachusetts Institute of Technology Press.

Allington, R.L., & Cunningham, P.M. (1996). *Schools that work:Where all children read and write.* New York: HarperCollins.

Allington, R.L., & Walmsley, S.A. (Eds.). (1995). *No quick fix: Rethinking literacy programs in America's elementary schools.* Newark, DE: International Reading Association; New York: Teachers College Press.

Anderson, R.C., Hiebert, E.H., Scott, J.A., & Wilkinson, I.A.G. (1985). *Becoming a nation of readers: The report of the commission on reading.* Washington, DC: National Institute of Education.

Au, K., Carroll, J., & Scheu, J. (1998). *Balanced literacy instruction: A teacher's resource book.* Norwood, MA: Christopher-Gordon.

Baker, L., Afflerbach, P., & Reinking, D. (Eds.). (1996). *Developing engaged readers in school and home communities.* Mahwah, NJ: Erlbaum.

Barr, R., Kamil, M.L., Mosenthal, P., & Pearson, P.D. (Eds.). (1991). *Handbook of reading research: Volume II.* White Plains, NY: Longman.

Cassidy, J., & Wenrich, J.K. (1998, February/March). What's hot, what's not for 1998. *Reading Today,* pp. 1, 28.

Chall, J.S. (1996). *Stages of reading development*. Fort Worth, TX: Harcourt Brace.

Cheek, E.H., Flippo, R.F., & Lindsey, J.D. (1997). *Reading for success in elementary schools*. Dubuque, IA: Brown & Benchmark.

Clay, M.M. (1993). *An observation survey of early literacy achievement*. Portsmouth, NH: Heinemann.

Cunningham, P.M., Moore, S.A., Cunningham, J.W., & Moore, D.W. (1995). *Reading and writing in elementary classrooms: Strategies and observations*. White Plains, NY: Longman.

Freppon, P.A., & Dahl, K.L. (1998). Balanced instruction: Insights and considerations. *Reading Research Quarterly, 33*, 240–251.

Gough, P.B., Ehri, L.C., & Treiman, R. (Eds.). (1992). *Reading acquisition*. Hillsdale, NJ: Erlbaum.

Heilman, A.W., Blair, T.R., & Rupley, W.H. (1998). *Principles and practices of teaching reading*. Upper Saddle River, NJ: Prentice-Hall.

Iversen, S. (1994). Balanced reading instruction: What children need to know and how to teach it. *Balanced Reading Instruction, 1*(1), 21–30.

Iversen, S. (1996). A metacognitive strategy approach to teaching reading: How appropriate and assisted instruction can help all children become readers. *Balanced Reading Instruction, 3*(1), 12–18.

Iversen, S. (1997). *A blueprint for literacy success: Building a foundation for beginning readers and writers*. Auckland, New Zealand: Lands End.

Iversen, S., & Reeder, T. (1998). *Organizing for a literacy hour: Quality learning and teaching time*. Bothell, WA: The Wright Group.

Learning to read and write: Developmentally appropriate practices for young children (A joint position statement of the International Reading Association [IRA] and the National Association for the Education of Young Children [NAEYC], adopted 1998). *The Reading Teacher, 52*, 193–214.

Pressley, M., Rankin, J., & Yokoi, L. (1996). A survey of instructional practices of primary teachers nominated as effective in promoting literacy. *The Elementary School Journal, 96*(4), 363–384.

Reutzel, D.R., & Cooter, R.B. (1999). *Balanced reading strategies and practices: Assessing and assisting readers with special needs*. Upper Saddle River, NJ: Prentice-Hall.

Spiegel, D.L. (1994). Finding the balance in literacy development for all children. *Balanced Reading Instruction, 1*, 6–11.

Spiegel, D.L. (1998). Silver bullets, babies, and bath water: Literature response groups in a balanced literacy program. *The Reading Teacher, 52*, 114–124.

Williams, K.A. (1993). Components of fluent reading: What influences are present? A pilot study. *Oklahoma State University Graduate Research*. Stillwater, OK: Oklahoma State University Press.

Williams, K.A. (1996). Reading assessment: Finding a balanced approach. *Balanced Reading Instruction, 3*(2), 1–14.

Williams, K.A. (1998). Balancing the books: Finding appropriate texts for information and instruction. *Balanced Reading Instruction, 5*(1), 44–45.

Author Index

Page references followed by *f* indicate figures.

C

Canney, G., 9, 22
Carbo, M., 104, 105, 107, 109, 114
Carnine, D., 132, 134
Carr, E., 156, 171
Carroll, J., 172, 181
Carter, M.A., 94, 103
Carver, R.P., 57, 69
Cassidy, J., 176, 181
Chall, J.S., 179, 182
Chambers, B., 135
Chandra, D., 63
Cheek, E.H., 175, 178, 182
Cherry, L., 52
Choi, S.N., 66, 69
Clapp, Patricia, 64
Clark, A., 65, 69
Clay, M.M., 76, 77, 78, 102, 145, 146, 170, 172, 182
Cleary, B., 54, 64, 67, 69
Clifford, E., 143, 171
Cole, J., 66, 69
Comprehensive Test of Basic Skills (CTBS), 124, 134
Conger, D., 65, 69
Conlon-McKenna, M., 54, 69
Cooney, B., 55, 69
Cooper, J.D., 38, 51
Cooter, R.B., 52, 175, 179, 182
Cormier, R., 64
Crawley, S.J., 31, 35
Creech, S., 57, 69
Crews, D., 59
Crossley-Holland, K., 62, 69
Cunningham, J.W., 177, 178, 182
Cunningham, P., 145, 170, 178, 181, 182
Cushman, K., 54, 64, 67, 69

D

d'Apollonia, S., 135
D'Aulaire, E.P., 61, 70
D'Aulaire, I., 61, 70
Dahl, K., 2, 7, 10, 23, 136, 168, 170, 172, 182
Dahl, R., 93, 103
Dalgliesh, A., 64
Davey, B., 40, 52, 170
Davis, F., 25, 35
DeAngeli, M., 64
Dechant, E., 29, 35
Deci, E.L., 141, 170
Deedy, C.A., 55, 70
Degen, B., 55, 70
Delpit, L.D., 10, 18, 22
Demi, 59, 70
dePaola, T., 52, 66, 70
Desai, L.E., 94, 103
Dickinson, E., 63
Diegmueller, K., 109, 114
Dishner, E., 28, 36, 147, 148, 160, 171
Dougall, J., 122, 134
Duffy, G.G., 52
Duffy-Hester, A., 2, 7
Durkin, D., 26, 29, 35
Dykstra, R., 10, 22

E

Ehri, L.C., 177, 182

Ekwall, E.E., 25, 30, 35, 45, 45*f*, 52
Esbensen, B., 63

F

Fairbanks, M., 26, 36
Feelings, M., 59, 70
Ferreiro, E., 77, 102
Fielding, L., 4, 7
Fisher, L.E., 62, 70
Fleischman, P., 64
Fleming, D., 55, 70
Flesch, R., 17, 22
Flippo, R.F., 175, 178, 182
Flood, J., 128, 134
Flood, S., 128, 134
Foorman, B.R., 109, 114
Fountas, I., 10, 22
Fountoukidis, D., 146, 170
Fox, P., 64
Frances, D.J., 109, 114
Freebody, P., 24, 25, 35
Freedman, R., 66, 70
French, M.P., 147, 171
Freppon, P., 2, 7, 10, 11, 22, 23, 136, 168, 170, 172, 182
Friedman, I.R., 65, 70
Fritz, J., 64
Fry, E., 146, 170

G

Gag, W., 55, 70
Galdone, P., 55, 70
George, J.C., 64
Gibbons, G., 59

Goble, P., 65, 70
Goodman, K., 128, 134
Goodman, Y.M., 113, 114
Gough, P.B., 177, 182
Greene, C., 66, 70
Greenewald, M.J., 77, 102
Greenfield, E., 65
Griffin, P., 108, 118, 135
Gunning, T.G., 31, 35

H

Hamilton, V., 62, 64, 65, 70
Hasbrouck, Jan E., 6, 116–135, 119, 122, 131, 135
Heiden, Delores E., 5, 72–103
Heilman, A.W., 4, 7, 29, 35, 106, 110, 114, 172, 178, 182
Heimlich, J.E., 147, 170, 171
Henk, William A., 6, 136, 137, 158, 169, 170, 171
Herr, S.E., 31, 35
Hiebert, E.H., 37, 51, 141, 170, 175, 181
Highwater, J., 65, 70
Hill, E., 59, 70
Hoban, T., 58, 59, 70
Honig, B., 105, 106, 110, 114
Hopkins, L.B., 63, 70
Huck, C., 152, 170
Hudson, J., 65, 70

I

International Reading Association (IRA), 178, 182
Invernizzi, M., 20, 23

Iversen, S., 2, 7, 41, 51, 52, 173, 174, 180*f*, 182
Ivey, G., 10, 11, 22

J

Jenkins, J.R., 24, 35
Jenkins, L.B. de, 65, 70
Jett-Simpson, M., 76, 77, 94, 102, 103
Johnson, D.D., 26, 35
Johnston, P.H., 77, 102
Juel, C., 26, 29, 36

K

Kagan, S., 158, 170
Kameenui, E.J., 132, 134
Kamil, M.L., 177, 181
Karegianes, M.L., 10, 23
Keepers, M., 158, 171
Konigsburg, E.L., 57, 70
Krementz, J., 66
Kress, J., 146, 170

L

Lapp, D., 128, 134
Lasky, K., 64
Lear, E., 63
Lebirman, D., 109, 114
Leibert, R.E., 57, 69
Leslie, L., 76, 94, 103
Levine, E., 86, 103
Lewis, C.S., 63, 70
Li, C.P., 105, 115
Lindsey, J.D., 175, 178, 182

Lipson, M., 138, 170
Livingston, M.C., 63
Lobel, A., 54, 58, 70
Logan, J.W., 4, 7
Long, S., 55, 70
Lou, Y., 128, 135
Lowry, L., 57, 63, 64, 68, 70
Lyons, C., 10, 22
Lyons, M., 65

M

Macauley, D., 67, 71
MacLachlan, P., 54, 70, 71
Maggart, Z.R., 106, 114
Mahy, M., 55, 70
Manzo, A.V., 106, 113, 114
Manzo, U.C., 106, 113, 114
Marinak, Barbara A., 6, 136, 137, 147, 158, 169, 170, 171
Martin, B., Jr, 55, 71
Martin, T., 52
May, F.B., 106, 114
Mayer, M., 83, 103
McCormick, S., 28, 35
McGee, L.M., 46, 48*f*, 52, 109, 115
McKeown, M., 4, 7, 24, 27, 35
McKissack, P. and F., 65
McMillan, B., 59
McPartland, J.M., 118, 135
Melnick, S.A., 169, 170
Melser, J., 78, 103
Meltzer, M., 65, 71
Merriam, E., 63
Merritt, K., 31, 35
Miles, M., 65, 71

Mohr, N., 65, 71
Moody, S.W., 135
Moore, D.W., 178, 182
Moore, J., 158, 171
Moore, L., 166, 171
Moore, S.A., 178, 182
Morgan, K.B., 108, 115
Morris, C., 152, 171
Morrow, L.M., 80, 103, 106, 115
Mosenthal, J., 143, 171
Mosenthal, P., 177, 181
Murphy, J., 71

N

Nagal, G., 128, 134
National Association for the Education of Young Children (NAEYC), 182
National Council of Teachers of English (NCTE), 178
Navy, D.M., 109, 114
Naylor, P., 56, 67, 71
Nichols, W.D., 4, 7

O

O'Dell, S., 64, 65, 71
Ogle, D.M., 46, 47*f*, 52, 156, 171
Opie, I., 60, 71

P–Q

Palincsar, A.S., 41, 52
Pallotta, J., 58
Pany, D., 24, 35
Parish, P., 55, 71

Paterson, K., 57, 64, 67, 71
Paulsen, G., 64
Pearson, P.D., 4, 7, 20, 23, 26, 35, 177, 181
Peck, R., 64
Pelletier, L., 141, 170
Perfetti, C.A., 24, 35
Pflaum, S.W., 10, 23
Pikulski, J.J., 105, 115
Pinnell, G., 10, 22, 150, 171
Pittelman, S.D., 147, 170, 171
Poremba, K.J., 109, 115
Porter, S.M., 170
Poulsen, C., 135
Prelutsky, J., 63
Pressley, M., 9, 23, 41, 52, 178, 182
Quackenbush, R., 71

R

Rankin, J., 9, 23, 178, 182
Ransome, J., 61
Rasher, S.P., 10, 23
Rasinski, T., 11, 23
Raskin, E., 171
Rathmann, P., 60, 71
Readence, J., 28, 36, 147, 148, 160, 171
Reeder, T., 174, 180*f*, 182
Reinking, D., 177, 181
Reutzel, D.R., 52, 175, 179, 182
Richgels, D.J., 46, 48*f*, 52, 109, 115
Robinson, N., 28, 36
Roe, B.D., 37, 51, 104, 114
Roehler, L.R., 52

Rosenblatt, L., 11, 23, 85, 103, 139, 143, 171
Roser, N., 26, 29, 36
Ross, E.P., 37, 51, 104, 114
Ruddell, R.B., 44, 52
Rupley, W.H., 4, 7, 29, 35, 106, 110, 114, 172, 178, 182
Ryan, R., 141, 170
Rylant, C., 57, 71

S

Say, A., 66, 71
Scheu, J., 172, 181
Schmitt, M., 10, 22
Schrader, Milly, 6, 116–135, 118–119
Schreck, J., 24, 35
Schumm, J.S., 135
Science Research Associates (SRA), 124, 135
Scott, J.A., 37, 51, 175, 181
Sendak, M., 54, 71
Seuss, Dr., 54
Shamat, M., 143, 171
Shanker, J.L., 25, 30, 35, 45, 45f, 52
Shinn, M.R., 131, 135
Silbert, J., 132, 134
Silverstein, S., 63
Simon, S., 67, 71
Slavin, R.E., 118, 128, 135, 141, 171
Smith, M.S., 105, 115
Snow, C.E., 108, 118, 135
Soto, G., 65
Speare, E.G., 64, 65, 71

Spearitt, D., 25, 36
Spence, J.C., 135
Spiegel, Dixie Lee, 2, 4, 7, 8–23, 52, 72–103, 176, 177, 182
Spinelli, J., 42, 52
Spiro, 37
Stahl, K., 2, 7
Stahl, S., 2, 7, 26, 32, 36
Stanovich, K.E., 105, 115
Staples, S.F., 67, 71
Steig, W., 56, 57, 71
Stevenson, D.L., 105, 115
Stotsky, S., 11, 23
Strickland, D., 9, 23, 39, 52, 107, 110, 115
Sulzby, E., 81, 103
Surat, M.M., 66, 71
Sutcliff, R., 64

T

Taback, S., 54, 71
Tafuri, N., 55, 71
Taylor, M., 64
Thompson, R., 108, 109, 113, 115
Thompson, Richard A., 4, 24–36
Thurstone, L., 25, 36
Tierney, R., 28, 36, 94, 103, 143, 147, 148, 160, 171
Tindal, G., 131, 135
Tolkien, J.R.R., 62
Tracey, D.H., 107, 115
Treiman, R., 177, 182
Truscott, D.M., 169, 170
Turner, R.M., 66, 71

U–V

U.S. Department of Education, 105, 115
Vacca, R., 11, 23
Vallance, Kerry M., 5, 37–52
Vallerand, R., 141, 170
Vaughn, S., 135
Venezia, M., 66, 71
Voigt, C., 64

W

Walberg, H.J., 10, 23
Walmsley, S.A., 177, 181
Walpole, S., 4, 7
Weaver, C., 108, 115, 146, 171
Wenrich, J.K., 176, 181
White, B., 109, 115
White, E.B., 57, 71
Wilder, L.I., 64

Wilkinson, I.A.G., 37, 51, 175, 181
Williams, Kathryn A., 1–7, 6, 172–182, 173, 177, 182
Wixson, K., 138, 170
Wood, K.D., 28, 36
Worth, V., 63

Y

Yep, L., 66
Yokoi, L., 9, 23, 178, 192
Yolen, J., 62, 71
Young, E., 59, 71

Z

Zelinsky, P., 59, 71
Ziefert, H., 52
Zintz, M.V., 106, 114
Zolotow, C., 61, 71

Subject Index

NOTE: Page references followed by *f* indicate figures.

A

ACHIEVEMENT TESTING, 130
ACTIVITIES: daily review, 146; learning, 31–34; with puzzles and squares, 31–34; student-centered, 24–36; teacher-directed, 24–36; vocabulary, 28–34. *See also* specific activities
AFRICAN AMERICANS, 64; roots and history, 65
ANANSI TALES, 62
ANDREW (CASE STUDY), 73–75, 85–94, 102; attitudes, habits, and interests assessment, 90–93; gathering and documenting information, 89–90; reading logs, 94; think-alouds during reading, 85–89; thoughts on books and reading, 91–93
ANECDOTAL EVALUATION, 133
ARABIAN NIGHTS, 62
ASIAN AMERICANS, 64; literature, 65–66
ASIAN CULTURE, 66
ASSESSMENT: anecdotal evaluation, 133; of attitudes, habits, and interests, 90–93; case studies, 72–103; informal, 99–101, 130–132; of literacy skills, 75–94; reading, 129–133
ATTITUDES, HABITS, AND INTERESTS: assessing (case study), 90–93
AUTHENTICITY, 12
AWARENESS: metacognitiveness, 44–45; of text structures, 158
AZTEC TALES, 65

B

BALANCE: between child development and literacy development, 54–56; concept of, 9; between literary forms, 57–58; programs that lack, 15–16; between range of reading and expectations about depth of reading, 67; between reading skills and literature, 56–57

BALANCED APPROACH: aspects of, 9–13; belief in, 21–22; definition of, 13; importance of, 13–16; perspective of, 8–23; suggestions for, 107–108

BALANCED BEGINNING READING PROGRAM: in culturally and linguistically diverse classrooms, 116–135; first year, 127–129; implementing, 116–126

BALANCED COMPREHENSION INSTRUCTION, 37–52

BALANCED LITERACY, 167; components of, 138–144

BALANCED READING INSTRUCTION: in action, 172–182; components of, 173; in elementary school, 136–171; in first-grade, 104–115; in grades 3–6, 154–166; in grades K–2, 144–153; history of, 108–110; how to establish and maintain, 20–22; kinds of, 175–179; philosophy supporting, 108; principles of, 2–3, 108–109, 173–174

BALANCED READING PROGRAM(S): achievement of purposes of literature in, 53–54; Beth's story, 110–113; characteristic of, 178–179; impediments to, 16–20; literature in, 53–71; planning, 119–123; rules of thumb for maintaining, 107; why we do not already have, 16–20

BALANCED VOCABULARY INSTRUCTION: with teacher-directed and student-centered activities, 24–36

BEGINNING BOOKS, 58–61

BEGINNING READING PROGRAM, 116–135

B.E.S.T. INTRODUCTORY PHONICS PROGRAM (BEST), 122

BETH'S STORY, 110–113

BIOGRAPHY, 66

"BOOK THINK," 68

BOOKS: Andrew's thoughts on, 91–93; beginning, 58–61; concept, 58; counting, 59; early, 59; high-quality picture storybooks, 60–61; information, 66; Mother Goose, 60; Newbery medal, 64; picture, 60; toy, 59; "word play," 146; wordless, 60

BOTTOM-UP CHANGES, 118–119

"BUDDY READING," 142

BURRUSS ELEMENTARY SCHOOL (MARIETTA, GEORGIA), 109

C

CALIFORNIA STATE FRAMEWORKS FOR READING, 123

CAP TEST. *See* Concepts about print (CAP) test

CARBO, MARIE, 112

CAUSE AND EFFECT MAPS, 46–47, 48*f*

CHANGE, 19

CHARACTER MAPS, 153, 154*f*

CHILDREN: balancing literacy development and their development, 54–56; matching with strategies, 21

CHINESE AMERICAN TALES, 66

CHOICE GROUP, 152

CLARIFYING, 42

CLASSROOM(S): balanced beginning reading program in, 116–135; balanced reading, 37–52; comprehension instruction in, 37–52; diverse, 116–135; elementary, 99–101; first-grade, 116–135; informal assessment in, 99–101; "integrated language arts," 150; "literature-based," 150; "whole language," 140–141, 150

COMPARE/CONTRAST ORGANIZERS, 164, 165*f*

COMPREHENSION: concepts important for, 138; graphic organizers as aid to, 45–47; instruction of, 37–52

COMPREHENSION CHART, 45, 45*f*

COMPREHENSIVE READING STRATEGY, 106

COMPREHENSIVE TEST OF BASIC SKILLS (CTBS), 124

COMPREHENSIVE VIEW OF LITERACY, 10–11; questions to help teachers gain, 20–21

CONCEPT BOOKS, 58

CONCEPTS ABOUT PRINT (CAP) TEST: Tyler (case study), 76

CONSTRUCTING MEANING, 139–140; in grades 3–6, 156–161; in grades K–2, 147–150

CONTEMPORARY REALISM, 63–64

COUNTING BOOKS, 59

CROSSWORD PUZZLES, 32–33

CTBS. *See* Comprehensive Test of Basic Skills

CULTURAL AND LINGUISTIC DIVERSITY, 126–127; balanced beginning reading program in classrooms with, 116–135

CULTURE: Asian, 66; Hispanic, 65; multicultural literature, 64–66; world, 61
CURRICULUM: consistent, 14–15; Distar Language I curriculum (SRA), 124; variety of, 12–13; vocabulary instruction in, 26–28

D

DAILY CHANGE, 19
DAILY REVIEW ACTIVITIES, 146
DECISION MAKERS: teachers as, 179–181
DEPTH OF READING: balancing range of reading with expectations about, 67
DETAIL MAPS, 47, 49*f*
DISTAR LANGUAGE I CURRICULUM (SRA), 124
DISTRICT POLITICS, 123–124
DIVERSITY: balanced beginning reading program in classrooms with, 116–135; cultural and linguistic, 126–127; of learners, teachers, curricula, and schools, 12–13
DOCUMENTING INFORMATION: Andrew (case study), 89–90

E

EARLY TOY BOOKS, 59
ELEMENTARY SCHOOL, 136–171; grades 3–6, 154–166; grades K–2, 144–153; informal assessment in, 99–101
EMERGING LITERACY, 106
EVALUATION: anecdotal, 133; of students' reading, 129–133. *See also* Assessment
EXPECTATIONS ABOUT DEPTH OF READING: balancing range of reading with, 67

F

FABLES, 61
FAILURE, 19
FAIRY TALES: example definition of, 152; French, 62
FANTASY: instructional framework for, 163, 163*f*; modern, 62–63

FICTION. *See* Historical fiction

FIRST-GRADE INSTRUCTION, 104–135; Beth's story, 110–113

FIVE-FINGER RULE, 142, 142*f*

FIX-UP STRATEGIES, 40, 140; continuum of, 160

FLEXIBILITY, 11–12

FLEXIBLE GROUPING, 140–141; in grades 3–6, 161–162; in grades K–2, 150–152

FOLK TALES, 62; example definition, 153; French, 62

FRENCH FOLK TALES AND FAIRY TALES, 62

FRY'S INSTANT WORDS, 146

G

GATHERING AND DOCUMENTING INFORMATION: Andrew (case study), 89–90

GLOSSARY: example definitions, 152–153

GO, ANN, 120

GRADES 3–6, 154–166; constructing meaning in, 156–161; flexible grouping in, 161–162; observations that define West Hanover's practices in, 161, 162*f*; reading strategies and methods in, 156, 157*f*; responding to text in, 164–166; text selection in, 162–164; words and word parts in, 154–156

GRADES K–2, 144–153; constructing meaning in, 147–150; flexible grouping in, 150–152; observations that define West Hanover's practices in, 150, 151*f*; reading strategies and methods in, 148*f*, 148–150; responding to text in, 153; text selection in, 152–153; words and word parts in, 144–147

GRAPHIC ORGANIZERS: as aid to comprehension, 45–47; word webs, 155, 155*f. See also* Mapping

GROUPINGS: choice group, 152; flexible, 140–141, 150–152, 161–162; for instruction, 125–126; interest group, 152; need group, 152

GUIDED PRACTICE, 41

GUIDED READING: in grades 3–6, 158–160; in grades K–2, 149–150; organizer for, 159, 159*f*

H

HABITS ASSESSMENT: Andrew (case study), 90–93

HERMAN LEIMBACH ELEMENTARY (ELK GROVE, CALIFORNIA), 116–135; anecdotal evaluation, 133; cultural and linguistic diversity, 126–127; district politics, 123–124; evaluation of students' reading, 129–133; first year, 127–129; program implementation, 124–126; program planning, 119–123; school profile, 117; top-down and bottom-up changes, 118–119

HISPANIC AMERICANS, 64; literature, 65

HISPANIC CULTURE, 65

HISTORICAL FICTION, 64; instructional framework for, 163, 163*f*

HISTORY, 108–110

HOUGHTON MIFFLIN LITERACY READERS, 123

I–J

IGNORANCE, 18–19

IMPEDIMENTS, 16–20

INDEPENDENT PRACTICE, 41

INDIANS OF SOUTH AMERICA, 65

INDIANS OF THE GREAT PLAINS, 65

INFORMAL ASSESSMENT: in elementary classroom, 99–101; implementation of, 101; results of, 99, 130–132; student reactions to, 99–100; teacher's questions about, 99–101; time management of, 100–101; where to start, 99

INFORMATION: gathering and documenting (case study), 89–90

INFORMATION BOOKS, 66

INSTRUCTION: balanced, 2–3, 24–52, 104–115, 119–123; comprehension, 37–52; first-grade, 104–115; frameworks for, 163, 163*f*; grouping for, 125–126; planning further, 174; reading, 106–108; strategy, 38–44; vocabulary, 24–36. *See also* Balanced reading instruction

"INTEGRATED LANGUAGE ARTS" CLASSROOMS, 150

INTEREST GROUP, 152

INTERESTS ASSESSMENT: Andrew (case study), 90–93

INTERFERENCE, 15–16; outside, 20

INTERNATIONAL READING ASSOCIATION: Balanced Reading Instruction Special Interest Group, 2; Exemplary Reading Program Award, 109

JACK TALES, 62

K

"KID WATCHING," 18
KNOWLEDGE: metacognitive, 174; vocabulary, 24–26
KOREAN LITERATURE, 65
K-W-L CHART, 46, 47*f*
K-W-L PLUS, 156–158

L

LATIN AMERICAN LITERATURE, 65
LEARNERS: assessing, 72–103; literacy, 72–103; variety of, 12–13
LEARNING ACTIVITIES: with puzzles and squares, 30–34. *See also* Activities
LEGENDS, 62; example definition, 153
LETTERS: characteristics profiled frequently, 145–146; identification of
    (case study), 76
LINGUISTIC DIVERSITY, 126–127; balanced beginning reading program
    in classrooms with, 116–135
LITERACY: balanced, 167; comprehensive view of, 10–11, 20–21;
    emerging, 106
LITERACY DEVELOPMENT: balancing child development and, 54–56; op-
    tions for promoting, 21
LITERACY INSTRUCTION. *See* Reading instruction
LITERACY PORTFOLIO, 94–98, 137; contents of, 95–96; goal setting, 98;
    management of, 96; ownership of, 97–98; selection of contents
    for, 96–97
LITERACY SKILLS: assessment of (case studies), 102; balancing literature
    and, 56–57
LITERARY FORMS: balancing and presenting, 57–58
LITERATURE, 53–71; Asian American, 65–66; balancing reading skills
    and, 56–57; extensions of, 68–69; high-quality, 56–57; Hispanic
    American, 65; multicultural, 64–66; purposes of, 53–54; tradi-
    tional, 61–62
"LITERATURE-BASED" CLASSROOMS, 150
LOGS: Andrew (case study), 94; commandments for, 164–166; options
    for, 166
LUM, JOYCE, 120

M

MAGIC SQUARES, 33–34, 34*f*

MAPPING: cause and effect maps, 46–47, 48*f*; character maps, 153, 154*f*; detail maps, 47, 49*f*; semantic, 30; story maps (case study), 82, 83*f*; word webs, 155, 155*f*

MAYAN TALES, 65

MEANING CONSTRUCTION, 139–140; in grades 3–6, 156–161; in grades K–2, 147–150

METACOGNITIVE KNOWLEDGE, 174

METACOGNITIVE AWARENESS, 44–45

MEXICAN AMERICAN STORIES, 65

MODELING, 41

MODERN FANTASY, 62–63

MODIFIED VOCABULARY SORT, 149

MOTHER GOOSE BOOKS, 60

MULTICULTURAL LITERATURE, 64–66

MYTHS, 61–62; example definition, 153

N

NATIONAL RESEARCH COUNCIL, 105, 108

NATIVE AMERICANS, 64; tales, 62, 65

NEED GROUP, 152

NEWBERY MEDAL BOOKS, 64

O

OBSERVATIONS: that define West Hanover's practices in grades 3–6, 161, 162*f*; that define West Hanover's practices in grades K–2, 150, 151*f*

ORGANIZERS: as aid to comprehension, 45–47; compare/contrast, 164, 165*f*; graphic, 45–47; for guided reading, 159, 159f

OTHER WORDS FOR... (ACTIVITY), 147, 147*f*

OUTSIDE INTERFERENCE, 20

OVERVIEW, 47, 50*f*

OWNERSHIP: of portfolios, 97–98

P-Q

R

READING STRATEGIES, 139–140, 140*f*; comprehensive, 106; in grades 3–6, 156, 157*f*; in grades K–2, 148*f*, 148–150; instruction in, 38–44; matching children with, 21

READING VOCABULARY: preteaching, 29

REALISM, 63–64

RECIPROCAL TEACHING, 41–44; strategies, 42

RECORDS: running (case study), 77–80, 79*f*

REEVES, BETH, 104, 109, 110–113

REFERRALS: special education, 132–133

RESEARCH, 10; on vocabulary knowledge, 24–26

RESPONDING TO TEXT, 143–144; in grades 3–6, 164–166; in grades K–2, 153

RESPONSE HEURISTICS, 160–161; format for, 161

RESPONSE LOGS: commandments for, 164–166; options for, 166

RESPONSIBILITY: parameters of, 142

RESULTS: from informal reading assessments, 130–132; screening, 124–125; from standardized achievement testing, 130

RETELLINGS: story (case study), 80–85

REVIEW: daily activities, 146

RILEY, RICHARD, 105, 108

RM. *See* Reading mastery program

RUNNING RECORDS: Tyler (case study), 77–80, 79*f*

S

SANDOVAL, DIANA, 120

SCHOOL VARIETY, 12–13

SCIENCE RESEARCH ASSOCIATES (SRA): reading mastery program (RM), 122

SCREENING RESULTS, 124–125

SEMANTIC MAPPING, 30

"SILVER BULLET," 177; search for, 16–18

SMITH, MAURINE, 120

SOUTH AMERICA: tales from Indians of, 65

SPECIAL EDUCATION REFERRALS, 132–133

SQUARES: learning activities with, 31–34; magic, 33–34, 34*f*

SRA. *See* Science Research Associates

U–V

UNITED KINGDOM, 108
U.S. NATIONAL READING SUMMIT, 105
VARIETY, 12–13
VENN DIAGRAMS, 46, 48*f*
VLP. *See* Vocabulary-Oral Language-Prediction
VOCABULARY: preteaching, 29; reading, 29
VOCABULARY ACTIVITIES: student-centered, 30–34; teacher-directed, 28–30
VOCABULARY DEVELOPMENT: environment that promotes, 139; independent, 138
VOCABULARY GOALS, 138–139
VOCABULARY INSTRUCTION: balanced, 24–36; in curriculum, 26–28; guiding principles for, 27–28
VOCABULARY KNOWLEDGE: research and background information on, 24–26
VOCABULARY SORT, 149
VOCABULARY-ORAL LANGUAGE-PREDICTION (VLP), 28

W–Y

WASHINGTON ELEMENTARY (ELK GROVE, CALIFORNIA), 129
WEBB, PATRICIA, 120
WEST HANOVER ELEMENTARY SCHOOL (PENNSYLVANIA), 136–171; balanced literacy components, 138–144; flexible grouping, 140–141; grades 3–6, 154–166; grades K–2, 144–153
WHOLE LANGUAGE CLASSROOMS, 140–141, 150
WHOLE-CLASS READING INSTRUCTION, 140–141
WHOLE-ONLY POSITION, 17
WIDE READING, 30–31
"WORD PLAY" BOOKS, 146
WORD WEBS, 155, 155*f*
WORDLESS PICTURE BOOKS, 60
WORDS AND WORD PARTS, 138–139; in grades 3–6, 154–156; in grades K–2, 144–147
WORLD CULTURE, 61
WRITING: Tyler (case study), 76–77
YOUNG AUTHOR'S FAIR, 98

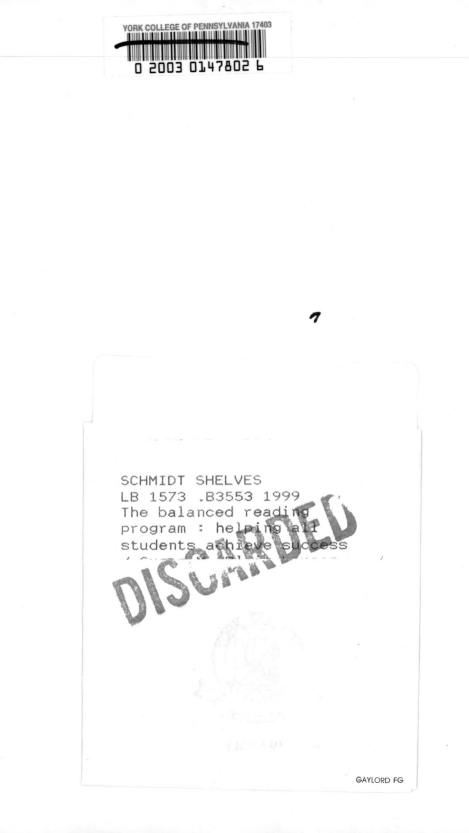